So You Want To Be A Manager?

by
Francis J. Bridges, Ph.D.

ESM BOOKS — DECATUR, GEORGIA

So You Want To Be A Manager?

Printing History
ESM Books trade paperback edition
1st printing June 1993

This book is available at special quantity discounts for bulk purchases for management training or educational use. Special programs using this book can be created to meet specific needs.

For details, write ESM Books,
Educational Services for Management, Inc.
235 E. Ponce de Leon Ave., Suite 307
Decatur, Georgia 30030

(404) 373-6386

Library of Congress Catalog Card Number 93-071312
ISBN 0-9623126-2-2
Printed in the United States of America

Contents

Preface

This book is dedicated to the millions of American managers who go to work each day to apply their skills. These are the people who make things happen, who assume more than average responsibility, who direct the use of economic resources, and who—more than any other group in America—shape the destiny of the United States.

The key to sustained growth of the economy without the erosion of inflation is greater worker productivity. Productivity is the quality and quantity of work output; and to be competitive in the newly opened world markets as well as in the domestic markets which are subject to foreign competition, American workers must be highly productive. It is the crux of management's role to stimulate employees to do a better job.

So You Want to Be a Manager? is a book designed to help influence the decisions of thousands of American workers who may become managers someday. It will help the newly appointed manager feel more confident about his or her work. And this book is an excellent review for any manager, regardless of tenure in management or level in an organization.

This book is not intended to be an academic treatise. It is written in understandable language to convey practical ideas to the manager in the real world. The approach used is one of common sense in applying basic principles and concepts to real life situations.

Finally, management is a subject that is easy to understand but difficult to apply well. Managers must be efficient (do things right) and effective (do the right things) for any organization to survive and prosper. Hopefully, this book will make the life of the practicing manager more rewarding and more successful.

On a personal note, I must give special acknowledgements to Ms. Libby L. Roquemore and the late Dr. David J. Schwartz.

Ms. Roquemore did the yeoman job of editing, proofing and correcting the manuscript. Her talents are in demand by many publishers and individuals, and her expertise was essential to the publication of this book.

The late Dr. David Schwartz, teacher and internationally known motivation speaker and writer, was a colleague for more than 30 years. His encouragement and enthusiasm for this book helped make it a reality.

Francis J. Bridges, Ph.D.
Decatur, Georgia

Part I: The Subject of Management

Chapter 1

What's It All About?

The greatest game in the world today is not soccer or baseball. It is being a manager! If you like thrills and risks, success and failure, action, and desire visibility, management is for you.

Of the 125 million people employed in the United States civilian labor force today, approximately twelve million are managers. These people live with excitement, work long hours, look forward to Monday mornings, and enjoy their work lives to the fullest. Managers who do not feel this way about their jobs are probably hanging on by their fingertips or one step away from unemployment.

Management is an activity of achieving objectives by working through "others." Working through "others" refers to the support personnel (at the first level of management these would be all nonmanagement employees) who report to their "bosses." Management personnel have many different job titles. Some are simply called managers; others carry such titles as supervisors, foremen, directors, executives, administrators, department heads, and many more. Some titles are tailored to the particular industry or type of organization. Whatever the title, all management personnel have the same task: working through support personnel to achieve the objective(s). One example of pure management is the football coach who works through eleven players on the field to achieve the objective—victory!

One point must be made clear now. A manager does not manage time, inventories, sales, money, operations, etc. *People who hold management positions manage only one re-*

source—people. Most job titles in organizations today are misleading. Such designations as Sales Manager, Inventory Manager, Office Manager, etc. may reflect other resources over which the manager has responsibility and control. But managers only manage people.

Chapter 2

Why Should You Go Into Management?

Maybe you shouldn't!

Many workers in the labor force are not qualified for management. They may be the best employees, but they may lose everything quickly if they accept a position in management. Being a manager is *not* for everyone.

The job, the title, more pay, and the added prestige may be a lure for a hardworking nonmanagement employee. Behind that appeal, however, are several traps.

What are the traps? Such things as better title, more pay, greater prestige, increased authority, much more responsibility, and possibly even a key to the executive dining room (or restroom).

These are positive incentives if you are prepared for a management career and willing to accept the risks that accompany such "perks." These same benefits, however, spell doom for the unprepared.

If you are not prepared to become a manager, you have three choices: Get prepared; postpone your decision until you are ready, or turn down the opportunity. It is better to have a decent job at which you are competent and highly regarded than to risk everything in a totally new world without proper preparation.

But you are ambitious. You feel your intelligence is not being taxed in your present job, and you desire the benefits of being in management. What should you consider next as you decide about a future in management?

5

Generally, those who go into management give reasons similar to the following. Check this list and see if you lean toward the challenge of a career in management:

1. If you demonstrate that you are a good manager, the opportunity for advancement is unlimited.
2. You gain greater respect and more status among your colleagues.
3. You get the chance to use more of your talents and skills.
4. Management offers the chance to acquire more authority (power) and responsibility.
5. The pay and fringe benefits are better in management.
6. You are confident you can manage as well as or better than the managers you have observed.

Chapter 3

Are You Sincere About a Career in Management?

If you think you are ready for the challenge of a career in management, answer the following questions. If your answers are positive, you are sincere about pursuing a career in management, and you have recognized some of the conditions which make management a challenge. It is a new world for those who have been in nonmanagement positions, and to accept the conditions is not always easy. *It takes a special type of person to succeed and be outstanding in the field of management, the most demanding of professional careers.*

Make this list of questions your starting point as you check your sincerity about that management career:

1. Do you like being in charge of other people?
2. Do you like to have the responsibility for the actions of others?
3. Do you think you could take satisfaction in seeing employees under your supervision succeed?
4. Would you like being judged on results—good and bad?
5. Would you like a job where your bosses have little appreciation for excuses?
6. Do you enjoy being a "team" player?
7. Do you like visibility?
8. Do you think you can lead others positively toward objectives and do so consistently?
9. Would you enjoy setting the model for employee conduct on the job?

10. Could you accept working 50-60 hours per week routinely when nonmanagement employees work 40?

11. Are you confident you know the subject of management and know what managers are supposed to do?

12. Do you thrive under a certain amount of stress caused by unusual demands, deadlines, schedules, and dealing with a multitude of different personalities?

13. Do you enjoy problem solving and decision making and the risks that accompany implementing your decisions?

14. Can you put aside personal interests and preferences and do what is best for the organization?

15. Can you handle pressure from your peers, your bosses, and your subordinates?

Chapter 4

How Are New Managers Selected?

Most new managers are promoted from within the organization from the ranks of nonmanagement employees. A less significant number are recruited from college campuses with an even smaller number of new managers coming from such sources as personnel placement firms.

The majority of new managers are employees who have had several years of work experience with an organization and have demonstrated the following:

1. Steady and dependable work habits;
2. Excellent knowledge and performance of their jobs;
3. The ability to get along well with others;
4. That they are not trouble makers, and
5. Loyalty to the organization.

Higher management would rather promote from within than chance the unknown qualities of newcomers who are strangers to the organization. Also, this provides an incentive to all employees who have a long-run desire to be in management.

Seniority, which is important in making job promotion, lay-off, and transfer decisions in nonmanagement employees, is not the most important factor in determining who goes into management positions. It does not dominate promotion considerations in management above the entry level position. *Performance is the key to climbing the management ladder once you are tapped for that first level position.*

Those management employees recruited from colleges normally go into a management training program before being assigned a permanent management job. Management training in these cases is most likely to be a course of several weeks or months designed to familiarize the recruit with all facets of the organization. This is not really management training! It is technical training which is important, but usually little attention is given to the actual subject of management.

You may wonder what recruiters look for in these college candidates. They seek to weed out the undesirable applicants for management jobs and select those who appear to be personable, highly motivated, possess good intelligence, and who show signs of interest in the organization on a long-term basis. They may look at such things as grades, extracurricular activities, employment records, academic major, and personal recommendations. Experience has shown, however, that managerial success is not guaranteed by an outstanding interview or high test scores. Neither can direct correlation be shown between I.Q. and academic success (or lack of it) and management effectiveness. Selection of management candidates also takes into consideration emotional maturity, stability, and whether the applicant is well-adjusted in general. Finding the answers to these questions about characteristics is difficult. Knowing the applicant well does not tell a recruiter if that person will make an effective practicing manager.

Other sources of management applicants are the mail, friends of employees, relatives of executives, and personnel placement services. Despite the questions and reservations about each method of selection, all of these have produced good and bad managers.

Regardless of the source of new managers, few are prepared to be successful. The solution to this problem is not being found within American organizations.

All of these routes remain open, however, to those who wish to enter the field of management.

Chapter 5

Is the Opportunity Unlimited in Management?

A job in management is the choicest career opportunity available. The only option that is more exciting is starting your own business. Even in this instance you are right back in management, but the difference is you are totally in charge of everything.

If a poll of 100 top executives were taken to find the number one problem in American organizations, I think the majority would say the shortage of competent management people. This may be the hi-tech age, the onslaught of the computer, the era of the specialist; but the *continued biggest problem, as it has been for decades, is the shortage of competency in management.*

Turnover in management is astronomical. It happens because managers retire, get transferred, resign, get fired, die, or are promoted upward. Opportunities abound. Where there is turnover, there is a vacancy. And every vacancy is an opportunity for someone.

If the idea of unlimited opportunity appeals to you, a career in management should be attractive. Heed the warning signs of high turnover, lifetime job probation, and total responsibility, though, and get yourself prepared. Management has pitfalls as well as opportunities.

The majority of managers are thrust into their first management position without any preparation. No wonder so many fail!

Chapter 6

Why Do So Many Managers Fail?

American managers tend to be intelligent, highly motivated, success-oriented people who are willing to assume additional responsibility and work unlimited hours. Yet, many fail. Why?

As a group, American managers perform professionally at each level in the organization. Certainly we would not have had the success as a nation we have enjoyed for generations without the outstanding executives, administrators, leaders, entrepreneurs, supervisors, etc. which populate American organizations leading the way. The challenge of management in the 1990's, however, is different.

Today, there is increasing organizational complexity, increased competition, voluminous governmental regulations, and a changed attitude among employees about their work and the work environment. *Quite simply, managers cannot get away with what they once could.* The tempo of the modern organization is much faster, and life styles of both managers and employees are vastly different.

The by-product of all this complexity is trouble for managers—both veterans and newcomers. The reasons they fail are different, however, and can be summarized by the two categories.

Veteran managers encounter the following problems:

1. Managerial obsolescence (the demands of the job exceed the skill and talent of the person)
2. Executive stress and burnout
3. Loss of support from higher management (reasons for

this vary, but it dooms the affected manager)

A different set of problems face the newcomer.

The most significant reason for failure is that few newly promoted managers have any training in management before assuming their management duties. This means that these new managers simply do not know what to do once they are in management positions. Many of them are promoted from within their organizations because of technical competence or outstanding performance in a nonmanagement job. There is no direct correlation between being a good worker and becoming an effective practicing manager.

These newcomers need knowledge of the subject of management plus some technical knowhow in operations, good human or personal skills, and the ability and background to evaluate and learn from each experience. The latter is not to be confused with On the Job Training, which often is nothing more than trial and error management and is a poor method of management training.

Beyond the lack of preparation for management positions, some of the more common reasons for the failure among newly appointed managers are the following:

1. They have failed to get the objectives clearly established by higher management.
2. They are not given enough authority to get the job done.
3. They are not accepted by their support personnel.
4. They are working against unrealistic goals and objectives.
5. They are working with impossible time standards for the completion of assignments.
6. They have personality conflicts with other managers (especially upper management).
7. They do not have the flexibility and adaptability to adjust to changing conditions.

Chapter 7

How Should New Managers Be Prepared?

How can an aspiring manager prepare to succeed in that first management job? The answer is the company can provide the training or the manager-to-be can begin a self-development course to program himself or herself for success when that opportunity knocks.

No organization employs typists, programmers, accountants, welders, or any other person for a skilled job without first testing for competency. *For some reason, however, American organizations promote or hire people for first level management positions without a firm knowledge of whether the employee can manage.*

Management at any level is the key to an organization's future. It is also difficult and challenging. Therefore, sending **prepared** managers into the ranks is the only way to gain an edge toward success.

Preparing employees for promotion into management should be a priority of all organizations. A program should include the following steps:

1. Supervisory management training conducted by a professional in the field of management training prior to starting the job;
2. An in-depth management orientation program before assuming management duties;
3. Follow-up supervisory management training and evaluation six months after the manager has had experience on the job; and

4. A directed program of reading and study in management.

If this type of training program is not available in your company (or is not yet available to you) and you still want to be ready for an opening in management, what can you do? *You can develop your own management training program.*

Caution must be raised at this point, however, because it is important for you to recognize that regardless of your preparation and knowledge, you may not become an effective practicing manager. Not every prepared person does, but you will increase your odds of success by being prepared.

Knowing a subject well and applying that knowledge effectively are two different things. But you must begin with the knowledge. Otherwise you will go into your first management position without the tools necessary to face the problems.

Begin your own self-development program by doing the following:

1. Go to a local library, a college library is best, and check out a basic management textbook. The year of publication is not important; just read it cover to cover.

2. Pick out two or three successful managers from different organizations and request an hour's time of each. Interview them with such questions as these:

    a. How did you learn to be a good manager?
    b. What tips and suggestions can you give me for getting prepared for a first level management position?
    c. What should I be most concerned about during my early days in management?
    d. What are some of the pitfalls you think I should watch for?
    e. Do you have any suggestions about how I can be a success in management?
    f. Which subject or activity do you think is most important in management?
    g. Do you have any philosophical tidbits or lessons learned in management which you can share with me?
    h. What has been your most troublesome area or

       your biggest weakness as a manager?

   i.   What is your greatest strength as a manager?

3.   Review the answers given to you in your interviews and develop a list of the most important points made. Go back to your basic textbook and review the material on these subjects. You may find extra, specialized management books on the topics considered most crucial by your interviewees which will add depth to your knowledge and preparation.

4.   *Write down your own ideas and mold them into a personal philosophy of management.* This is what will be a major influence on your behavior and actions when you become a manager.

5.   Finally, while on your current job, evaluate everything around you and learn from all of it. Watch other managers as well as your own boss to see how they operate. A keen observer can learn from the very personal style of other managers. You will acquire a background of knowledge to help you learn and grow with each experience.

Chapter 8

How Does Training in
Management Give You an Edge?

*True training in management is invaluable to the new
manager or management candidate.*

Training in management will include such subjects as the
following:

1. How the American economic system works
2. The basic concepts of management
3. The fundamental functions of a manager
4. Organizational behavior and communication
5. Problem solving and decision making
6. Personal growth and career development
7. Motivation skills and human relations techniques

These are the most significant topics. Each of these subjects includes dozens of sub-topics, concepts, and principles.
Part II of this book lists and describes 101 practical points in
management to help you get prepared.

How does this kind of training in management give you an
edge?

Simply, if you receive professional management training,
you acquire the following:

1. Familiarity with management jargon
2. A body of knowledge that allows you to learn from
   your daily management experiences
3. Greater confidence in your actions as a manager
4. Stimulation of your thinking about your job

5. New ideas and techniques which you can consider, adapt to your needs, and apply

Consider the topics carefully. Imagine going into your first management job without any of this knowledge or any ideas on these subjects. *Almost 98 percent of new managers take the plunge into management without first receiving management training.*

Don't you think you will have an "edge" if you learn something about the subject of management first?

Ideally, your employer should provide additional management training after you have been on the job about six months. The second phase of training allows you to pursue subjects in much greater depth. You can stress the importance of problem solving and decision making. This second phase also allows you to step back and reflect on your experiences as a manager during the initial six months. Then, you can evaluate your strengths and weaknesses and dedicate yourself to being a complete professional for the remainder of your career.

If your employer does not offer any of this management training, you should seek it for yourself. Local colleges, trade associations, industrial management clubs, and many other groups or organizations offer management training programs. Costs vary from nominal to very high, lengths of programs range from a few days to several weeks, and all of the programs have some merit.

Your investment in your future will pay off in big dividends in your career advancement. *Without question trained managers have an "edge," but there are still no guarantees that they will stay on top without continuing growth and development as a way of life.*

Chapter 9

What Role Does Professional Management Orientation Play?

If you are going to act like a manager, think like a manager, and be a manager in every way, you should begin doing so the first day you are a manager. Professional management orientation insures that you are completely management oriented when you start that first job in management. You cannot carryover attitudes and ideas from nonmanagement when you become a manager.

The purpose of any management orientation program is to give you insight into the real world of management. It should be done by your employer; but if it is not, there are actions you can take to compensate. The end result should be the same: You are prepared to meet the demands of management in a way that is satisfactory to your employer and in a way that will give you a better chance for success.

If you find you are conducting your own management orientation program, these subjects are the ones you should discuss, in depth and detail, with your supervisors before your job begins:

1. The role of the modern-day manager
2. The rights, authority, and liabilities of the manager
3. The history of management in your organization
4. The real *mission* (expectations) of managers
5. The total responsibility of managers
6. The importance of your job in the total scheme of things

7. The importance of you as the individual performing the management job
8. The further growth of the company and your opportunities in management in the future

These subjects are essential to a management orientation program, and you should have a full understanding of each point prior to beginning the job.

Ideally, your organization should provide this program with a professional person conducting the sessions, formalized content, tight control over the administration of the program, and complete agreement by you and your employers of what your job entails. If there is no program in your organization, you must take the initiative and seek the same information and points of agreement yourself. You will be glad you did because you will have taken another step in underwriting your future as a successful manager!

Chapter 10

Should You Have Your Own Personal Philosophy of Management?

Every new manager feels somewhat lost when first starting that management job. After all, you are in a new world with different kinds of problems and drastically changed responsibilities. Furthermore, expectations are great, and you have no background of experience on which to rely. You can see that such emotions as inadequacy, insecurity, and worry (perhaps even fear) would not be unusual. As time goes by and you weather some management storms, your confidence gradually builds. Eventually, you will learn what you can and cannot do, what works and what doesn't, and what your managerial strengths and weaknesses are. From that point on, you begin to manage with more assurance.

A personal philosophy of management on which you can rely helps you and veteran managers most when dealing with daily problems and making decisions. Managers who behave inconsistently in their dealings with people or who appear to be running scared when confronted with problems undoubtedly do not have a personal philosophy of management.

A personal philosophy of management consists of your fundamental beliefs, basic concepts, convictions, and firm ideas about management. Since management involves achieving objectives working through others, many of your beliefs about management will concern people (your employees). Your managerial philosophy also could include values relating to the organization, to yourself, to customers, stockholders, your bosses, and any other factor which influences your management decision making process.

The importance of having a personal philosophy of management is that it influences every action you take and all decisions you make leading to consistency in your behavior as a manager.

Part of your managerial philosophy might be the following:

1. Every decision I make will be in the best interest of the organization.
2. I will strive to be totally fair-minded and objective when handling employee problems.
3. I will base every action I take on all of the available facts.
4. I will take full responsibility for the work of any of my employees.

Fundamental beliefs and ideals like these provide much strength and confidence to a manager when dealing with hundreds of problems and decisions.

New managers should begin early to write down those ideas, beliefs, and concepts which he or she believes are most important in the daily practice of management. Not having a managerial philosophy is like managing with your eyes closed and your ears plugged!

Chapter 11

What Is the "Charge" to Managers?

If you decide that a career in management is for you, remember that the *great managers are only a little bit better than the average ones.* There is not a whole lot of difference between excellence and mediocrity, but that slight variance makes the big difference over time.

Strive to develop yourself to the fullest by acquiring all of the knowledge you can in the field of management. Mix this knowledge with experience on the job, and then evaluate your experiences to learn from doing. *Great employees like professional managers tend to be developed over time on the job.*

You can expect to make many mistakes no matter how prepared you are for a career in management. Do your best to space your mistakes and grow and learn between them. Concentrate on improving your managerial techniques in all areas of management. Accept criticism positively and keep your attitude positive.

Take full responsibility and look for more. If you have ambition to "go to the top," do not balk at promotional opportunities. If you have employees who are not motivated, not excited about their jobs, or who make costly mistakes, guess what? The blame lies with you!

If you like excitement, risks, and organizational adventure, you are going to find it as a manager. But, *even if you fail in one organization, you may succeed in another.* It has happened often, *but you must have the fundamental ability and skill as a manager mastered so that you did not fail because you were unprepared or lacked management know-how.*

If you do well in management, you will be doing a great service to your employees, bosses, and to yourself. Indirectly, you will also benefit consumers, owners, and society in general.

Good luck to you in your managerial career!

Part II: The 101 Most Important Practical Points in Management

Introduction

The following "101 Most Important Practical Points in Management" have been acquired from talking with managers from all parts of the United States, from consulting experiences, from research, from observation, and from management literature.

The purpose of these 101 points is to help you, the new manager or the aspiring manager, learn more about management. They will help you understand better the rules of the management game and provide you many ideas that can be adopted as part of your personal philosophy of management. Your familiarity with these practical points should give you more confidence as you begin your career in management.

Do not mistake these points for answers to organizational problems! All the points have much validity and should be reviewed often, but management is an activity with no textbook solutions or pat answers.

The "101 Most Important Practical Points in Management" are organized and presented in seven categories.

The first category is about the fundamentals of management. These are basic concepts which provide a quick overview of what management is all about. These points are the rules of the management game.

The second category is about management in general. These points reflect on the activity that we identify as a professional discipline.

The third category is about managers themselves. Many tips are included in these points to influence "how" a manager should perform, and many of the points characterize successful managers.

The fourth category deals with employees. An effort is

made to present points that will give you a better insight into the toughest of all jobs - managing people. A number of management myths are dispelled in this category, and many good "people" tips are presented for your review.

A fifth category deals with planning and control. These important managerial activities are keys to organizational effectiveness and achieving objectives. Review these points many times and remember that poor planning is the number one cause of organizational failure.

The sixth category is about the function of organizing. This is the least familiar subject to most managers. Acquiring managerial soundness in this area helps give you an edge. Most daily management problems stem from bad organization structure, and the most important points and principles of organization are included for you to study and review.

Finally, the seventh category deals with communication. A manager must not only communicate with others, he or she must do so effectively. The points in this section deal with improving communication skills and knowing the channels of communication.

Successful managers have basic beliefs and well thought out ideals which influence their day to day decision making. This produces managerial consistency which pleases employees and bosses alike. Acquiring managerial consistency may take time, but the best way to begin is to develop a personal philosophy of management. These points are designed to form the foundation of a personal philosophy.

You will want to add to these points as you gain experience. Keep your list of ideas and principles handy for quick referral. A new idea may just be the thing to stimulate your thinking and influence you to take the right course of action in a difficult situation.

Here are 101 ideas to inform you, stimulate your thought processes, and support your managerial goals.

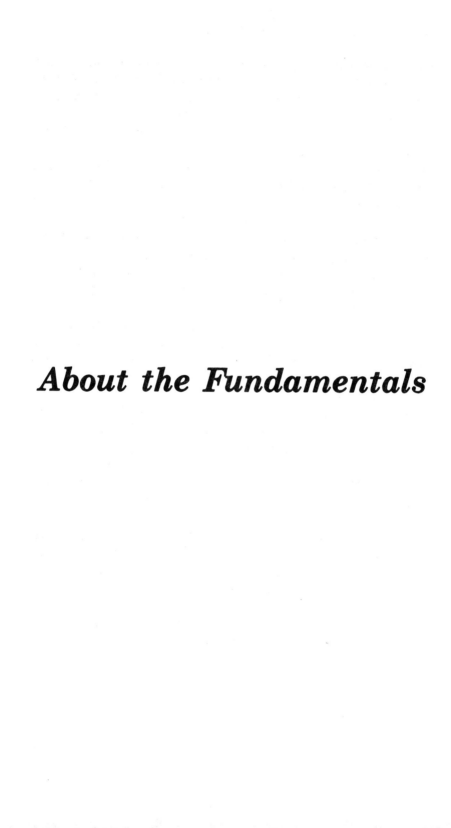

About the Fundamentals

Management Is People Oriented

The activity of managing is one involving people. In a formal organization these people are the employees who report directly to you, the manager. Whether you have one or two or thirty or forty employees reporting directly to you, your job as a manager is to achieve pre-determined objectives working through them.

Managers have many resources under their responsibility, authority, and control, including people. **But** the only resource one manages is the people!

You don't manage sales, inventories, budgets, an office, production, etc. You manage people!

Thus, many job titles such as sales supervisor or office manager are misnomers in business today.

Management Is a Basic Process

All managers have the same main functions, duties, or responsibilities. Although the identification of these may vary in number depending on your source, the following are generally accepted as essential responsibilities:

To Plan
To Organize
To Implement
To Control

Every manager may not be a sound planner, organizer, implementer, or controller, but the requirements of the manager's job dictate these fundamental responsibilities.

A new manager should learn everything possible about each of these functions and realize that each consists of many subactivities.

When you are involved in planning, organizing, implementing, and controlling, you are engaged in the basic process of management. **And the process goes on continuously forever!**

The Synergistic Management Concept

Here is the true **mission** of managers.

Every new manager especially should know and understand the management mission prior to entering the management ranks.

The word *synergy* means the end result is greater than the sum of the parts. In simple arithmetic lingo, 2 + 2 = more than 4.

Applied to the job of a manager, the real mission becomes one of directing the use of resources in such a way that, over a period of time, the manager creates an end result which is far greater in value than the starting values of the resources combined. If managers cannot do this, they will eventually be replaced or the organization will fail.

Managers Are Totally Responsible

Of all the points a new manager should become familiar with, the Total Responsibility Concept is the most vital. The concept states that a manager is absolutely, totally responsible for everything that happens, good or bad, from his or her position in the organization downward. This responsibility begins the first day you are in the job.

A manager is employed to work on behalf of another manager above him or her (the boss). In the manager's area of supervision, often referred to as the scope of responsibility, no matter what problems occur, no matter how much success is achieved, and no matter the nature of the activity, that immediate manager is responsible.

The total responsibility concept wipes out excuses. If you

are the person in charge, the manager, then you are the one responsible for **everything** from your position downward. You cannot shift the blame nor fault those below you for the failure to attain results. Some management prospects shrink from this kind of responsibility, and they refuse to be promoted into management positions because of it.

Being a manager is not for everyone. Not all employees, no matter how good an employee they are, want the additional responsibility that accompanies supervising people and directing the use of organizational resources.

Managers Are Judged on Results

Managers are judged on results (performance). If not, managers would be judged on years of service, personality, how hard they try, how many hours they spend in the office, how well liked they are, and on and on. None of these mean anything unless combined with the successful completion of the assigned objectives.

Although there are exceptions to all concepts, the majority of organizations do attempt to judge managers on performance. This is sound and fair as long as

1. All managers know clearly what their objectives are, and
2. Higher managers making the judgments are fair-minded and objective in their evaluations.

Many decisions made today cannot be judged fairly until enough time has elapsed to know the results.

Management Is by Objectives

For a supervisor to manage as efficiently and effectively as possible, every employee must know what to do, when to do it, and why his or her work is important. This is best achieved when the whole organization manages by objectives.

Management by objectives requires the organization to state clearly and in writing the following:

1. The primary objectives (why the organization exists)

2. The operating objectives (annual or twelve month objectives)
3. Unit objectives (annual objectives for divisions, branches, departments, etc.)
4. Individual managerial objectives
5. Individual nonmanagement employees' objectives

The idea is that if every employee, every manager and every unit (part) of the organization achieves its objectives in the given time period, the operating or twelve month objectives of the organization as a whole will be reached. Achieving these objectives keeps the organization in line with the pursuit of the primary objectives.

Written objectives not only give direction to the efforts of all parties involved, but also they can become the basis for evaluating performance. Written objectives coupled with time standards form the basis of a sound control program to insure that overall performance is on schedule and that costs are within the budget.

Lack of clear-cut written objectives for each person and part of the organization causes disjointed and uncoordinated effort and leads to waste and inefficiency.

Management Is Decision Making

The most common activity in management is decision making. Every manager makes decisions, good or bad, and stands on the results. Decision making is an unavoidable responsibility that leads to action. This action, multiplied by every decision made, brings about the results which are the goal of the manager's job.

Most decisions in management are subjective in nature and involve problems that include people. These are called *general management problems*. Nonpeople problems or technical problems can be difficult, but they represent only about ten percent of a manager's total problems.

Decision making is not very scientific and many factors affect how a manager acts under certain circumstances. Mathematical decision making is used in some organizations if the variables in the problem can be quantified. But this is not always the case and such precise decision making is therefore limited in use.

A general notion is that the best management planners tend to be the best decision makers who in turn tend to be the best managers.

Management Is a Science

There is a small part of management that can be called a science. It is an important part of management, but most aspects of management should be considered an *art*. Management may be studied as a social science, since it involves the interrelationships of people. Much research about the whole subject of management is taking place now, and a large body of literature is available with research findings, valid principles, and concepts. All of this points toward management as a *science*; however, management is *not* an exact science.

The science of management is the application of the scientific method to general management problems leading to problem solving and decision making. Although the use of the scientific method in problem solving and decision making does *not* guarantee a right answer or perfect solution to a problem, it *does* increase the percentage of right answers over time. A general management problem refers to any kind of problem in the organization about any subject as long as people are part of the problem - which only encompasses about ninety percent of all management problems!

The scientific method as used by managers is a practical, uncomplicated approach in seven steps. The first step is the most important because it dictates the direction of your analysis. Your analysis of management problems should be in writing unless there is an urgency for a quick decision.

The steps in the scientific method are the following:

1. Clearly identify the fundamental management problem;
2. List all the facts pertinent to the problem;
3. List alternative courses of action to solve the problem;
4. List advantages and disadvantages of each alternative;
5. Review all of the above;

6. Draw conclusions, make recommendations and/or decisions, and

7. Follow up or check to determine if the decision made has brought about the desired results

Using this approach does not guarantee your answer or decision will be right. It does force you to consider the facts, review alternatives, and be more logical and objective in your analysis than if you made decisions on hunch, intuition, emotion, tradition, etc. It is a sound approach that is used in government, business, the military, and by others when making major decisions. This approach is also called subjective decision making.

The use of the scientific method by managers, even in a limited way, is what makes part of the activity of managing a science.

Management Is an Art

Most of the activity of managing is an *art*. The artistic part of management is how one uses his or her acquired knowledge of the subject and job experience. It is the application of the sum total of all this knowledge and experience to a given situation to bring about the desired results. The emphasis is on "how" or the "way" you do something.

Management styles and techniques are as varied as the number of managers. Given the same decision to implement, ten different managers will cause ten different results. This is because of the "way" managers do things - the *art*.

Every practicing manager is an artist who performs every day in front of employees, bosses, peers, vendors, customers, etc. Yet, every manager is so different in background, experience, education, perception, training, and knowledge that each will manage differently. This adds to the need for managers to be judged on results. Any individual manager should be free to perform in his or her own way as long as there is no violation of company policies and the philosophy of higher management is maintained. The bottom line is results not method!

Management Is the Significant Difference

Every organization has competition. If you are part of a business firm, you have much head-on competition. Even the United States Postal Service has competition. There are few monopolies left.

When you review successful organizations in a highly competitive field, you wonder why some are more profitable or successful than others. If they provide about the same services or similar product lines and the prices do not vary much, you invariably wonder what makes the difference. You wonder because inevitably one organization *is* better than the others.

The significant difference between competing organizations originates in the hundreds of decisions managers make over a period of time. Decisions in any organization flow downward and create action which results in change. Changes affecting pricing, styling, merchandising, packaging, advertising, customer services, location, efficiency, product lines, and hundreds of other things over time make the significant difference between competing organizations. All these change-initiating decisions have one common factor: the managers who made and implemented them. It is the quality of those managers' decisions that makes the critical difference.

About Management Generally

The Universality of Management Concept

Henri Fayol, a Frenchman, pioneered study and research in the field of general administration in the 1920s. He originated the universality of management concept. The theory is that any manager in any kind of organization, located anywhere, will engage in the basic process of management (planning, organizing, implementing, and controlling) as he or she works through people to achieve objectives.

The fundamental concepts of management do have universal application. Managers around the world do have the same major responsibilities. The difference in management, one company to another or one nation to another, rests in the styles and techniques used by individual managers as they plan, organize, implement, and control; and in the different attitudes, cultural disparities, values about work, etc. that employees bring to the workplace.

Managers Need Three General Skills

Practicing managers need many special skills. By category, however, the most general skills needed are the following:

1. Technical,
2. Human or personal, and
3. Conceptual

Technical skills means that you understand the details of the job. You know procedures, operations, methods of doing the work, and the many specifics that are part of a supervi-

sor's responsibility. If you are overseeing the work of opera-
tive employees, you need to know their jobs, be able to train
and correct them, plan work schedules, and understand the
relationship of work in your area to other work performed in
the organization. An essential skill for first-line supervisors
and most middle managers is this type of technical knowhow.

Human or personal skill refers to a manager's ability to relate effectively with other employees, groups, departments,
peers, and bosses so that desired objectives can be attained.
Examples of good human skill would be the ability to communicate effectively, provide sound leadership to your employees, and **most importantly**, be able to get along well with
others in the organization. This is an absolute requirement for
supervisors and all middle managers.

Conceptual skill is considered to be the rarest of all management skills. Much like the general of an army, a manager
must plan, lead, decide, and act at all times in terms of what
is best for the total organization. Plans and decisions must be
made that override individuals and vested interests. The
health of the whole organization takes precedence over any individual or any part (department, division, branch) of the organization. Top managers must be able to see this "big picture" and to do that they must have conceptual skill.

Managers Are Uncommon People

Once you go into management, you become different! You
are no longer "one of the gang," and you may even lose some
of your friends if you have been promoted from within. Becoming a manager requires an adjustment in your behavior
and your thinking. Management is full of responsibility, high
expectations, and **pressure**.

All your thoughts as a manager must be centered on what's
best for the organization. You, the manager, are the "company" to nonmanagement employees. And don't think that
every statement you make and every action you take is not
being observed by your employees! They won't miss anything!

These changes from nonmanagement to management make
you "different." You have new, greater responsibilities; you
have authority; your perspective is different; indeed, your

world is different. This makes you a vastly different type of person from the ordinary employee. You are now part of a group called the "uncommon."

As you move upward in the management ranks, you become even more different, more uncommon, than the nonmanagement employee. You may advance high enough to be considered humorously **abnormal!** This means you have achieved managerial success, but people like you are few in number.

Professional Managers Share Few Traits

Individuals in management are uniquely different, yet there are a few personal traits common to the successful professional managers.

First, research has shown that successful managers are more **opportunistic** than nonmanagers. They take advantage of situations which arise and try to capitalize on them. This is not to imply that they seek personal gain at the expense of others. Rather, they visualize opportunities in company problems, they generate ideas to improve conditions, they plan continuously for the future. These are the kinds of things that an opportunist in management does.

Second, research indicates that successful managers are better at differentiating between facts and opinions and that they draw wiser inferences from observations. All of this suggests that successful managers tend to have better perception and judgment than nonmanagers. Having this ability helps a manager make sounder decisions which is the heart of the manager's job.

Third, successful managers are highly motivated about their work, their organizations, and their future careers. Being highly motivated alone is no guarantee of management success. Motivation added to knowledge of your job and proper direction toward worthwhile goals is required, however, to reach your objectives on time in an effective and efficient way.

Although these traits are found in many successful managers, the "personal trait theory" should *not* be used to select people for management jobs. This theory, which holds that management selection should be based on the candidate's having a select number of personal traits which are supposedly common to other successful managers, does not cover enough territory. The reason is that many more actions than opportunistic behavior, sound judgment, and high motivation make up a manager's job. Every veteran successful executive has his or her own management technique, which is largely different from any other person's. It does not hurt to develop these traits, because they are common to most successful managers and they are valuable traits to have, but they are not the only ones you will need.

Education, IQ, and Success in Management

Advanced education and having a high IQ are not requirements for success in management. If you possess a college degree and if you have a high IQ, congratulations! But, neither of these things guarantees success in dealing with people, making sound decisions, being creative, planning properly, etc. Most of managing is an "art" which cannot be taught in school. Being bright or having a high native intelligence does not necessarily produce stability, high motivation, or the human skills needed to work with and through people. In fact, the highest IQ in an organization may belong to a secretary or a shop worker, not a top manager.

Management is so complex that it is hard to isolate any single characteristic as a true key to success. You need to be smart enough to get the job done and know enough to minimize mistakes. No one is handicapped in management by lack of an extensive education or an IQ in the genius range. Willingness to learn, hard work, dedication to professional goals, and good common sense are qualities that lead to success in management.

Professional Managers Control Time

Professional managers at any level know the value of controlling "time." Since time is the one resource we cannot recapture, recycle, or reconstruct, it becomes our most important nonhuman resource.

Obviously time passes whether we are productive managers or not. We have the choice about the use of time. We can squander it, or we can control and use it for personal and organizational gain.

Sound planners tend to make better use of time than others. Managers who plan carefully always project time standards along with objectives. Planners attempt to visualize the future, prepare for possible problems, and reach desired goals within a set time frame in the most effective and efficient manner.

You have probably heard people say, "I'd like to do that but I don't have enough time." Usually when such a statement is made, the individual is either a poor planner or badly organized.

Time is too valuable a commodity to waste. It is too valuable a commodity to fill with mediocre effort.

Control your time carefully with check lists, control charts, and time checks. Set time standards for doing something at a "level of excellence." Then, when you have more free time, enjoy it to the fullest, produce even more, and find you can do all those things you did not have time for before.

In management, time equals money. The manager who makes the best use of time normally will be regarded as the most efficient manager.

Discriminate Your Way to Competency

The word **discriminate** has taken a beating over the past thirty years. Laws tell us what discrimination can lead to in society, and the punishment for breaking antidiscrimination laws has much of the business community on edge all the time. There is, however, a positive side to this word, and every professional manager must know it.

If you are a manager, it is good to discriminate between good employees and bad, between sound decisions and risky ones, and between what actions are good for the organization and those that are wrong. All managers should be discriminating. What's bad about discrimination, and what gets you into trouble, is when you let biases prejudice the decisions. This can occur when the subject pertains to employment, promotion, or reward of employees on the basis of sex, age, race, religion, or national origin. This is really not a problem if you adopt competency as the standard for making these kinds of decisions.

The most qualified applicant should be employed and the most productive employee should be promoted and rewarded. Forget the questions of sex, race, religion, and national origin. Go with the employees who are overall the most highly qualified to do a particular job and who, by their performance, deserve promotion and recognition.

Remember, your decisions should be made in view of what's best for the organization. This should override individual prejudices and biases at all times.

The Reflective Phenomenon

In management circles, the reflective phenomenon occurs when the supervising manager has a strong or dominant personality. This figure may be the president of the organization or a first level supervisor or both. The phenomenon is that individuals surrounding these strong personalities, managers and nonmanagers alike, will tend to adopt that person's mannerisms, personal habits, and even the style of management.

Every new manager should learn from experienced managers; but you want to be individuals, not mimics, in management style.

Be objective in your evaluation of other managers and borrow only the best points, discarding the rest. Every manager should be different, and all management styles are different. Use what you pick up, but make it yours. Don't be too influenced by the dominant boss or strong personalities of managers around you, no matter how successful they are. Their ways won't necessarily work for you.

Managers Can Sink or Swim

Approximately 98 percent of all new managers are promoted into their jobs without any management training. This is the unconscious "sink or swim" approach taken by higher managers who control promotions.

Why this is the way it is no one knows! This has been the practice of most American organizations since their beginning. Without question, the job of the manager is the most complex and demanding job in the entire organization. No other specialized position would be filled in the organization without some test of competency or extensive preparation being given the candidate.

If you are given the opportunity to go into management, request management training first. If training is not offered or available, then develop your own management training program (review Chapter Seven for details).

Get prepared to be a manager or plan to "sink." If you don't sink, you will probably end up "dogpaddling" (barely staying afloat) in management most of your career.

Number One Economic Waste

When you get into management, be careful not to fall into one of the major traps that characterize average (synonym of mediocre) managers. The trap is doing part of the work your employees should perform. When fifteen dollar per hour managers do the work of six dollar per hour employees, there is a waste of nine dollars per hour. Multiply that by real wages and you can see the scope of the economic waste.

Your job, by definition, is to achieve the objectives of the organization by working **through** others, not **for** others. Your job is to see that the work is done properly and on schedule, not to do the work yourself.

Emergency situations and crises will occur occasionally which demand everyone's efforts to complete a job or accomplish the desired results. This sort of involvement by a manager should be an exception and not a rule. And proper planning should all but eliminate these situations.

Think about the purest management situation: the football coach. He will incur a strong penalty if he loses control and runs out on the field to make a tackle. Instead, he develops eleven others (players) who can and will execute the plays while he stands on the sidelines. This is the real job of the manager.

Professional Management Orientation Is Essential

Have you heard the expression, "Give me a break!" That should become the war cry of new managers who are promoted into management without professional management orientation.

Professional management orientation refers to the provision of a highly organized, well-conceived orientation program that lasts for several days, includes all new managers, and stresses subjects such as the following:

1. The new manager's mission
2. The total responsibility concept
3. The importance of the job
4. A history of the company
5. The philosophy of the organization's management
6. Why you were selected - your importance
7. The Company's organization structure

All of these topics and more (review Chapter 9) should be part of the formal management orientation. If a new manager is not properly conditioned when he or she enters management in the organization, then all of his or her ideas are likely to be acquired from others whose attitudes and information may be poor.

Developing a professional management team requires planning, time, and attention on the part of any organization. If a company wants a positive spirit of professionalism among its management team, it must have a program of professional management orientation. The program should begin for you, the new manager, prior to the first full day on the management job. This is the way to achieve a unified effort among all management team members, and leads to mutual respect for each other.

Managers Tend to Be Underpaid

Normally when you get promoted to management, you get an increase in pay. This is one of the incentives that attracts people to the field. The increase in pay is exciting, but it alone is hardly reason enough to accept a manager's job.

When your review the demands on managers, the risks, the total responsibility, being judged on results, the long hours, the pressure, the deadlines, and the problems with employees, then pay (and increases in pay) fades as a reason for a career in management.

Many top level managers earn spectacular salaries on the surface, but the risks of their jobs are so great and the longevity in the position so brief on average that annual income may not be as high as it appears.

The point to keep in mind is that management is a performance oriented world. Adequate compensation for a job done well **follows performance.** Don't expect to be over-compensated in advance of your contribution to the organization. For this reason, managers tend to run behind others on pay schedules.

Be careful of managers who have the attitude that "when they pay me more, I'll do more." These people are "losers" and are likely only temporary employees in management.

Management Training Is a Three-Step Process

Once you settle into your management job, you should consider picking one of your employees to become your replacement in the future. Sound peculiar? It is not. Over time you can share your knowledge and experience with this person and give him or her added responsibility so that, when an opening in management comes, this person will be ready to step into it. It could be your position when you move up, or it might be another position in the organization. One-to-one tutoring of this type may be the best of all management training if the tutor is a real professional!

While you are training a replacement, you should be receiving instruction and guidance from a manager above you so that, when the opportunity arises, you'll be ready to assume a higher management job.

The objective of this three-tier approach is to have highly competent managers at every level in the organization and to have someone prepared, trained, and **ready** to move up whenever a need arises. If the new manager can do the job as well as or better than the predecessor (you), it reflects even more positively on you than your own performance in that position alone.

Always Do a Benefit/Cost Analysis

The objective of every decision a manager makes is to do what is best for the organization. This means that the return or **benefit** from your decisions or actions must be greater than the **cost**. This concept implies that return and cost be measured in more ways than just money.

The cost of something may be in the employees' feelings, your loss of face, a decrease in morale, the lack of assurance provided to customers, and so on. This is in addition to monetary concerns. The benefit of something may be measured by improved employee attitudes, higher morale, less turnover and absenteeism, more satisfied customers, and content stockholders, etc., in addition to a greater monetary return above costs.

Much of your actions/decisions as a manager are based on subjective analyses. In these cases you don't have all the facts, but you must act anyway. You cannot always measure the effectiveness of a decision in dollars and cents, especially immediately.

Regardless of the circumstances, the manager should **never** forget that the objective of his or her decisions is to try to effect a result far greater in value than the cost.

"Average" Is an Unacceptable Standard

The term "average" is a totally undesirable word when used as a standard of performance in American organizations. It is a condemnation when applied to an employee. No one wants to work for an average company, be considered an average employee, or receive average pay.

As a new manager, you want to supervise work that is considered the **best**; you want to work for a **leading** company; you want your employees to be **excellent** workers; you want to be on the **number one** team; you want to set goals that are **outstanding**.

This attitude depicts a great manager, not an average or mediocre one.

Professionals in management set high standards and goals and work doubly hard to achieve them.

This is what sets them apart. They never settle for **average** performance as the standard of expectation—in themselves or in others.

Management's Mistakes Are Fodder for Unions

Most American managers would prefer not to deal with unions if they had a choice. The reasons are simple: Unions force management to adjust to an agreed upon union-management contract with all of the provisions and rules regarding employees' wages, promotions, grievances, working conditions, etc. Stated explicitly, unions cost management much of its flexibility and part of its control over operations.

The first union in the United States began in 1792. After nearly 200 years of existence, the union is not likely to vanish. Both unions and American business management, however, must abide by the provisions of the Taft-Hartley Act, the major legislation controlling union and management activity in the United States.

Why does the union continue to exist and in some industries grow? *Because of management's mistakes!*

Managers often mishandle employees, make poor decisions regarding wages, changes, standards, work methods, etc. without proper planning and careful consideration of employees' interests before implementing a decision. Management may act arbitrarily with one group of employees or even an individual, and the result is a demand for representation by a union so that the rights of employees may be outlined and protected. Since unions may be "voted-in" by a majority of the certified employees, they may also be "voted-out" by a majority of the certified employees. Elections are authorized and supervised by the National Labor Relations Board (NLRB).

Is is unfortunate that some employees receive needed recognition, status, and a sense of belonging from the local union rather than from the company that employs them. The needs of the employees should be provided by the company via the supervisor on a daily basis. Once again, remember that unions thrive on management's mistakes!

Get Ready for Stewed Supervision

As a new manager, you should be aware of the number one game played in America. It is called "grandstand quarterbacking," and to play you merely have to criticize anyone who does anything. It can be your superior managers in the organization, officials in government, the Pope, or even the coaches and players on a sports team. It is a healthy game to play when kept in proper perspective, but it is played regularly whether healthy or not!

To the new supervisors, here is a word of caution about playing this game. You are going to be discussed! Your employees will observe every move you make, every reaction you have, and hear every word you speak. They may criticize all of it. When something occurs that affects them significantly and you have been part of the action, you will most likely be *roasted*! You will be on the table that evening (and perhaps for many evenings) as the main dish—"stewed supervision!"

Be prepared for this kind of criticism and don't let it get the better of you. Listen to it, and turn positive and negative criticism into constructive suggestions for improving your job performance. Above all, recognize the game and your natural role in it, and don't overreact.

Learn to Avoid Managerial Obsolescence

There is much turnover in management. This creates a wide world of opportunity for the new manager. Managers retire; they get promoted, transferred, fired, sick, and some die while employed. Something else happens to managers, too, which you must be aware of. It is *managerial obsolescence.* Beware of becoming obsolete in your management job.

Managerial obsolescence occurs when the demands of the job become greater than the skill and/or talent of the individual who holds the position. You do *not* have to be promoted to become obsolete.

Obsolescence can set in when a manager fails to stay in touch with advanced technology; when he or she cannot adjust to a new type of employee; when reorganization has changed the way the manager must operate; or it can happen when new top management has different, perhaps greater, expectations and demands. There are other ways to become obsolete, but the idea is that you must not rest on past performance.

No matter how effective you were as a manager in the past, don't rest on your "laurels!" Management is a dynamic environment; and you can become obsolete anytime conditions change and you do not adjust.

About Managers Specifically

Managers Make Things Happen

When you observe the real professionals in management, you note immediately that they are action oriented. They are self-starters. They make things happen. These managers know where they are going, what needs to be done to get there, and when to do things. These managers are enthusiastic about their work. They are creative and motivated to achieve. Anticipating results generates enthusiasm.

Remember the three types of people in the world:
1. Those who make things happen;
2. Those who watch things happen, and
3. Those - the **overwhelming majority** - who have no idea what has happened!

Without question, professional managers are among those who make things happen.

Managers Must Be Aware

When you go into management for the first time, you are likely to be awed by the fact that the experienced managers seem relaxed, confident, and positive enough to enjoy their work. On the other hand, you, as a novice, may be swamped by the responsibility of your job, the complexity of decision making, the people problems, and the constant time pressure facing you.

The underlying factor which makes these experienced managers seem relaxed and confident in the same world you find stress-filled is **awareness**.

Developing awareness is a conscious activity. You plan a program to determine the answers to questions about the organization, about activities, about personalities, about future projects, etc. Externally, you seek answers to questions about your industry, general economic conditions, political actions and the resultant impact, world affairs, etc.

Gaining this information in a systematic, deliberate fashion averts the panic of being suddenly uninformed when you need to have all the information available. Being more informed allows you to view your job and your work more objectively. You have a better perspective.

Awareness is not the same as having all the answers. Awareness is identifying activities, people, events, and statistics, and then making your value judgments in an unfrenzied state. All of which leads to improving your odds of making a sounder decision. An informed, more aware manager should develop better plans, make sounder decisions, and feel more comfortable about the future.

There is no excuse for being uninformed - not knowing what's happening inside and outside the organization. Spend at least ten minutes each day staying current on everything, asking questions, reviewing the economic and political news. It is a great investment of time in your future.

Managers Can Be Turtles or Hares

One of the great lessons to be learned in management is that steady performance on the job will be much more impressive than occasional bursts of brilliance.

Organizations and departments that are outstanding have managers who are productive on a daily basis not once in a while or just when a major project deadline is approaching. Steady attention to the problems at hand and consistent progress toward achieving objectives are characteristics of professional managers.

Organizations like managers they can depend on day in and day out. They like managers who are reliable, productive, and positive every day.

New managers should strive to develop this kind of stamina and consistency in their job performance.

Managers Are on Lifetime Probation

Most new managers don't realize they are on lifetime probation. Usually it is not mentioned in any interview; it is not in the employee handbook; it is not covered in orientation, nor is it posted on the bulletin board. It is a well-guarded secret that should be made public.

Most organizations have probationary periods for new non-management employees that range from thirty days to six months. This probationary period is well-publicized and strictly enforced in most cases.

New managers are not on probation for a certain number of days, months, or years. Managers are on probation from the first day onward. They never get off probation! They may retire after forty years or be fired or quit after one week. They were on probation their last day on the job just as they were on their first.

Regardless of the seniority, a manager has no guarantee of employment except that assurance which may be gained from repeatedly demonstrating competency on the job.

Managers Must Wear the Management Hat

Whether you begin your career with a position in management or are promoted into management from a nonmanagement job, you will have to adjust your attitude. You will have to think and act like a **manager**.

You, as a manager, are the "company" to your employees. What you say, do, don't say is the company. One of your major responsibilities is to act and speak in the best interest of the organization. For this reason, you should associate with managers, think like a manager, act like a manager, and in every way *be* a manager.

This does not imply that you can have no friends among nonmanagement employees. It simply means that they should know and you should know that every decision you make as a manager is going to be in the best interest of the organization. Sometimes these decisions may override friendships.

Maintain your friendships at all levels, but be sure you wear your management hat twenty-four hours a day.

Managers Are Physically Healthier

Managers are physically healthier than nonmanagers, based on days absent from work each year due to sickness. Nonmanagement employees are absent, on the average, six times more per year for illness than managers.

Why is this true? The answer is simple. When managers get up in the morning, every morning, they know that other people are depending on them at work. They know that decisions are in process that they are a part of. They know that excuses are unacceptable. They know total responsibility is theirs, and they know they will be judged on results. They know they cannot afford to be absent from work for routine reasons or minor illnesses.

Furthermore, managers tend to be much more excited about their jobs and more interested in their work than nonmanagers. **They want to go to work.** Everyone should feel this way, but unfortunately not all employees do.

Managers Should Be Surrounded by the Finest People

One of the real secrets of being a great manager is that you are only as good as your employees. Have highly trained, highly motivated, dedicated and loyal employees, and you have a great manager!

There is no greatness or real professionalism in management if the employees are average or mediocre.

Since everything employees do reflects on managers, it behooves a manager to develop every employee to his or her full potential. Doing this benefits the employee, the manager, and the company. Only after you adopt this standard of excellence as part of your management work do you have a chance to become a real professional in management.

Every Manager Has an M. O.

Whether admitted or not, every manager like every court-room attorney, every professional criminal, and every concert musician has his or her own M. O. (*modus operandi*) or method of operation. A manager's M. O. is a description of the manager in action. It portrays the manager's predictable patterns of behavior as he or she works with and through people to achieve objectives. The M. O. would include expected reactions to problem situations and the individual techniques and habits observed in daily supervision.

Ideally a manager's M. O. should match his or her personal philosophy of management.

The best way to obtain a manager's M. O. is through employees. Request the employees of the manager to write a description of their boss - in complete confidence and anonymity. Have the employees include all the noticeable strengths and weaknesses of the manager and omit nothing. From these individual accounts, develop a composite profile of the manager. This is that manager's M. O.

The only value in developing a manager's M. O. is for improving managerial effectiveness. The M. O. should be compared with the manager's personal philosophy which details how he or she **thinks** he or she is performing as a manager. If the comparison shows variances, changes will need to be made to improve managerial performance.

Just what changes to make and how much variance to accept are questions that each manager must explore in the on-going attempt to improve his or her managerial effectiveness.

Managers Set the Tone and Example

An often overlooked responsibility of new managers is that of setting the tone and example for the employees you manage. Setting the tone refers to the "spirit" of the work group.

Establishing a positive attitude toward work, generating an air of enthusiasm, and creating a sense of importance about the work being done are examples of positive "spirit."

Setting the example for other employees to follow relates to absenteeism, work habits, being on time, having a positive attitude toward higher management and the company, and actions that demonstrate company loyalty.

It is unlikely that your employees will be the ideal types of workers in attitude and behavior unless you set the example and lead the way.

Management Is One on One

One of the best tips for a new manager to remember is that although you may be in charge of eight, ten, or twenty or more employees, you manage each *one at a time.*

Managers have group meetings, departmental discussions, and make decisions that affect whole groups of employees; but the activity of managing effectively is best done one on one.

The reason for this is that every employee is different. The job needs, responses to stimuli, and perception both of you as a manager and the work situation vary greatly from one employee to another. You can see that managing everyone in the same way when each employee is so different would lead to frustration on your part and theirs, and ultimately lack of effectiveness as a manager.

Managers Need a Personal Style of Management

Although much has been written about styles and types of managers, there is no one best way to manage. Benevolent, autocratic, democratic, participatory, Theory X, Y, and Z are only a few of the "styles" of management. What every manager needs is his or her own **personal style of management**.

You can and should study and observe successful managers. You will find that they are different in virtually every respect:

personality, technique, background, experience, manner in handling people. Yet, if you judge these managers on results, all are successful.

You can watch and listen to managers and read on the subject of management. You can discuss philosophies and styles of management with others. In the final analysis, however, you will succeed or fail on what you do as an individual. So develop your own style!

Imitation may be the greatest form of flattery, but it is no shortcut to management success. Concentrate on maximizing your personal assets and minimizing your shortcomings as you evolve a style of management that suits you.

Your style of management will be uniquely yours. It will also be subject to change when circumstances and situations dictate. Underlying your personal style, however, should be a consistency that your employees can count on. Employees need the sense of security you provide as a manager when you deal with them in a consistent manner regardless of the changing problems and situations you face.

Be a Non-Conformist Who Knows When to Conform

Most progressive organizations like managers who are alive with ideas, who challenge the old ways of doing things, who produce many viable suggestions and proposals, and who seek added responsibility. This type of manager is also a trouble maker to other organizations. It is precisely this type of non-conformist manager who has paved the way for progress in American business, but not every organization wants one. It depends on the attitude and philosophy of the organization.

If your organization encourages the above action, then enjoy the opportunity to be different and develop your skills at innovation and creativity. But never forget the cardinal rule that says, *know when to conform!* There will always be guidelines or limits of acceptable behavior for managers in every organization. Exceeding these limits is foolish and dangerous for your career in management.

When you get into management, find out immediately what

the rules of the game are. Determine what your limits will be and what the boundaries are. Especially, find out what higher management encourages lower managers to do. You may not like what you uncover and subsequently change organizations, but you may also map yourself a road to higher management by steering well within the borders while fulfilling your maximum potential.

Management's Most Embarrassing Moment

When problems in a manager's area of supervision attract the attention of higher management and higher management investigates, that manager had best know all about the problem. If not, he or she has just suffered the most embarrassing thing in management - being caught unaware.

This would never happen if every employee were educated, conditioned, and programmed to keep his or her immediate boss informed of any unusual action taking place.

Managers must control their work group, know what's happening at all times, and accept the responsibility for all of the action, good or bad. There is no excuse or defense for not being on top of everything going on in your own area of supervision.

Management's Most Difficult Situation

The most difficult thing in management happens when decisions are handed down by higher management to be implemented by lower management. When these decisions are made at the top for the purpose of benefitting the organization, but they conflict with what lower management would like to do personally or thinks is best for the organization, then the lower manager has his or her most difficult assignment.

The job of the manager is to do what is best for the organization. Often what one manager thinks is contrary to the thoughts of another; however, your job also is to respond to the direction and orders of managers above you whether you totally agree with the decisions or not.

Examples of these kinds of situations include the following:

1. Being instructed to cut the size of the labor force;
2. Reducing operating budgets;
3. Skipping or postponing an expected wage hike, and
4. Scrapping a project that has a lot of potential.

It is a true test of a manager's mettle to handle these situations; but if professionalism is your goal, you must learn how to put these decisions into effect with the least amount of disruption to your employees.

Leadership Is Badly Needed in Management

Not every manager is an effective leader and not all effective leaders are in management. Ideally an organization would like every manager to be competent in the knowledge and practice of management **and** also possess and demonstrate effective leadership.

Being a leader in a management job is different from being a competent, knowledgeable manager. A competent manager with good leadership skills generates the "extras" that make some departments outstanding in performance while others are good or average (remember average is undesirable).

Effective leadership creates employee loyalty, pride in work, an *esprit de corps*, a willingness to volunteer for overtime work, a positive attitude toward the company and fellow employees, and job satisfaction.

There is a shortage of effective leaders in every kind of organization. When you go into management try hard to develop soundness in management and also become an effective leader. Read and study about people and leadership, and glean ideas you can use in practice to enhance your professionalism in management.

Little Things Make a Big Difference

Remember this statement when you go into management. Nothing is more true than the fact that managers who are the best do things a little bit better than the average. This small difference separates the "excellent" from the "mediocre."

Becoming a real "pro" in management requires improvement in all of your areas of supervision over time. But improvement tends to be gradual, **almost subtle**, not sudden or startling. You may not observe much difference in other managers on a daily basis, but you'll see a big difference in end results.

Your objective should be to strive to improve your planning skills, decision making techniques, your ability to communicate effectively, your leadership ability, etc. a little as you gain experience. Work hard to improve slightly in the dozens of areas of management, and you'll be amazed how that small improvement multiplies in the end results.

One or two seconds separates first place and second in a 500 mile speedway race. One stroke can be the difference between first place and second in a major golf tournament. A baseball player who hits .300 gets only one more hit every ten times at bat than a .200 hitter. Yet, the difference between the end result is as if one wins by hours, dozens of golf strokes, or ten hits out of ten at-bats. That same disparity holds true in management. Little improvements make a **big** difference.

Gaining the Personal Edge

In Part I, Chapter 8, we talked about management training giving the newly appointed manager the competitive edge. As important as management training is to your career, it requires time to digest and time to learn to apply the wide variety of information you acquire. In the short run, what can you do to gain the personal edge toward making you stand out as a new manager?

The answer is simple and yet overlooked by many. There are three things you can do which will enhance your image as an employee and a manager in any organization.

First, when you are given an assignment, *begin to do it immediately!* The fact that you don't delay, procrastinate, don't question the assignment, and act immediately is always impressive to bosses.

Next, perform the assignment *on time!* Nothing makes a better impression than to do a job on schedule (or ahead if possible) without grumbling, and with enthusiasm.

Finally, make certain you *do the assignment well!* Strive for exceptional quality in every task you perform. After all this is what you expect of your employees as a professional manager, and you should deliver no less to your managers.

In summary, when any employee performs an assignment immediately, on time, and does it well, in time that employee stands out as a true professional. This kind of performance on a consistent basis gives you the personal edge.

About the Employees You Manage

Develop Employees to Their Fullest

Of all the factors of production only "people" can grow and develop into something more valuable than they were originally.

Managers have a major responsibility to develop employees to their fullest. This is a twenty-four hour a day job.

Since people are the number one resource of any organization, a number one priority of every manager is to guide, direct, educate, train, inspire, stimulate, and encourage all employees to grow and develop to their maximum potential.

The benefits of this are obvious. The employee becomes more valuable and will either gain more job security, a promotion, or both. The manager benefits because all employee efforts reflect on him or her. Finally, the organization benefits from having a more productive and valuable employee.

It is economically and socially sound to develop employees to their fullest. You do this through practicing positive leadership techniques and professional management.

Make Perfectionism a Disease

The definition of management includes working "through others" to achieve objectives. It is a totally people-oriented activity. Management is also a largely inexact science full of risks, uncertainty, and the unpredictable behavior of people.

Any manager at any level who expects or demands perfection from employees is living in an unrealistic world. It is professional to aim high, to encourage the perfect job, to strive to maximize profits and minimize costs, but mistakes and errors are bound to occur. There are too many variables which managers cannot control and cannot foresee with pinpoint precision to expect perfection.

Perfectionism is a disease that destroys people. Keep standards high, but as a manager learn to adjust to the imperfections of your employees, peers, and bosses. And learn to adjust to the imperfections in *you.*

Know Your Personnel

If you ask managers the question: Do you really know and understand your employees? Most will say, "Yes." If a third party talks confidentially with the employees about how they think about their jobs, the company, what they want, need, and desire from the job and company, then often you get a different set of answers from those given by managers.

When this is the case, and it too often is, there exists a conflict area between management's thinking and that of the employees. The employees and the managers are on different wave lengths. What results is management bases its employee relations efforts on what it **perceives** not what employees truly think and feel.

Do you think this could cause problems? You better believe it does!

When managers take action based on their concept of employees' needs, interests, and desires and the expected results are disappointing, then management has proved they really do not know their employees as well as they think. Every manager should work hard to understand each individual employee.

Know your personnel! Talk to them, seek their thoughts, try to draw out their needs, wants, and desires as employees under you. This will help you minimize internal problems in the future.

Settle for Nothing But the Best

There should be two types of employees, excellent and "ex." Unfortunately nearly every organization has many ordinary, average employees. These employees are performing in a manner no better than minimally acceptable. Organizations also have marginal employees - the ones barely holding their jobs. Then, organizations have a few employees they can call **excellent**. These employees are the "pros." They are dedicated, motivated, productive, and loyal to the organization.

Since every organization has a few excellent employees, why do you think every job is not filled with excellent employees? Why should any organization settle for less than the best when it comes to employees?

The excuses you hear go like this: Those excellent employees are hard to find and keep. They just are not available. Things are different today, people don't feel the same about work as they used to. The unions and the government encourage mediocrity.

The truth is the "great" or "excellent" employees have never been "out there." The unions and the government do not condemn excellence. Managers have to take the responsibility themselves for average or marginal employees, just as they must take the credit for creating "excellent" employees.

The source of the vast majority of excellent employees is right there in the ranks of current employees. Ordinary employees can become *extraordinary* under the direction, training, education, leadership, and inspiration of a professional manager. The job takes time, but developing people is an essential part of the job of a manager. If some employees resist growth, don't want to become extraordinary, and wish to remain mediocre; then, when conditions are right, replace them with people who do want to grow.

Managers as well as organizations are judged by the performance of their employees. Learn to recognize the factors of excellence in your employees, and strive to instill the desire for excellence in them all.

Don't Confuse Seniority with Competence

Seniority refers to the length of employment a person has had with the present organization. Length of employment or seniority is used widely in American organizations as a basis for job promotion considerations and salary increases, and, when necessary, layoffs of nonmanagement employees.

Seniority has little place in management. Years of service is important as an indicator of loyalty, but it should never be confused with competency in the individual. People can work for twenty years and simply repeat the first year of experience nineteen times, or twenty years seniority can be the sum of twenty years of solid experience. Time is not the differentiating factor, competency is.

In management, the person considered most qualified to perform a job is usually promoted or transferred, etc. The action is taken to benefit the organization, but it is rarely made on the basis of seniority.

Union-management contracts nearly always require that seniority be considered in most decisions about employees (such things as promotions, layoffs, raises, vacations, etc.). Union members believe in using seniority because it is objective, can be easily understood, and is simple to apply. Managers, however, are not subject to this kind of seniority protection. Competency is the rule for survival and promotion in management.

Seniority does not exclude competency, but you must learn to make the distinction. You must make that distinction, when allowed to do so by work agreements, upper management, etc., in your decisions about employees' promotions, salaries, work assignments, transfers, and dozens of other cases.

Employees Have Job Needs, Wants, and Desires

When you first go into management, you will meet all of your employees. These people consider you their "boss." To you these people are "support" personnel. Over time, they will try to figure you out. You should be doing the same with each of them.

To help you solve the mystery of stimulating your support personnel consider these facts: Every employee has basic job needs, wants, and desires; and when these basic job needs, wants, and desires are not satisfied to a reasonable degree, the employee becomes a problem or quits (and make no mistake an employee can quit and leave the company or quit and still be on the job!).

Every manager has the challenge of understanding each employee. Since each employee is different from the next, then every employee should be managed differently. To do this, you need to know what the basic job needs, wants, and desires of each employee are. You do this by listening, asking questions, engaging in discussions, exchanging ideas and thoughts with your employees over time.

Some of the more common job needs, wants, and desires of employees are job security, higher pay, opportunity for advancement, better working conditions, recognition, better supervision, etc. When an employee's job needs, wants, and desires are not satisfied to a reasonable degree, you as the manager have a disgruntled employee. The individual employee determines what is reasonable, not you the manager. You can watch for signs of dissatisfaction such as absenteeism or tardiness, more mistakes or sloppy work performance, frequent complaints about most everything, perhaps some diffidence or even belligerence toward you and other managers, and the ultimate signal - resignation from employment.

Every manager will do a better job of working through people if he or she really makes a conscientious effort to understand each individual employee and reasonably satisfy the basic job needs, wants, and desires.

Learn the Value of Empathy

Empathy is defined as putting yourself in the other person's place. Having empathy is a positive characteristic of managers who really care about communicating effectively. Psychologically the manager who can consider the feelings and attitudes of employees before he or she talks or writes to them will do a better job of getting a particular message across. Trying to understand how people feel and think before praising, criticising, or delegating work to them allows a manager an opportunity to select a method of communication and a form of communication that should be more effective.

Putting yourself in the employee's place tells him or her that you place a high value on employees' needs and feelings.

It tells your employees you are concerned with doing whatever is necessary to communicate more effectively and get along more smoothly with them. It gains their support for all you try to accomplish when you begin your tenure with them in this manner. You find your employees more cooperative, supportive, and productive when they believe you genuinely take their feelings into consideration in your day to day management decisions.

The Three Kinds of Job Income

Every employee receives three different kinds of income on the job.

First, the employee receives *monetary* income. This is the total dollars and cents per payday we enjoy talking or even bragging (or complaining) about.

Second, the employee receives *real* income. This is what can be bought in goods and services with the monetary income. This kind of income really measures an employee's standard of living. It doesn't matter how much monetary income you receive, it is what you can do with it that counts.

Finally, the employee receives *psychic* income. This is the psychological satisfaction from a job. This kind of income is just as important as monetary or real income in terms of creating job satisfaction, preventing employee turnover, and boosting employee morale. Psychic income can be given or received from a pat on the back, a nice raise, verbal praise, special responsibility assigned, a promotion, a new title, a bigger office, etc. The important point to remember is that whenever any employee receives less than enough of any of the three incomes, he or she is likely to leave the organization or at least be looking and waiting for a chance to leave.

You as a manager can make sure that a satisfactory level of all three incomes is maintained. Lack of psychic income can cause as much turnover as lack of monetary income.

Learn to judge when to give psychic income for maximum benefit and don't deflate its value by overdoing it.

The Correlation Between Morale and Productivity

Morale is the outlook an employee has at any given moment about his or her work environment. The work environment includes the working conditions, the supervision, the opportunities, the job security, the wages, the recognition given, and so forth.

Most managers believe there is a strong positive correlation between morale and productivity, i. e., the higher the morale, the better the performance of the employee. With a few exceptions, this tends to be true.

The exceptions occur largely when recession, business failures, and layoffs cause large scale unemployment. Those remaining employed in the hardest hit industries tend to have low morale, but they produce more, work harder, and strive to remain employed. Here morale is low, but productivity is high.

In general, American managers invest considerable time and money trying to improve the morale of their employees so that they will be more satisfied with their jobs and, in turn, achieve and maintain high job performance.

How Pay and Performance Correlate

One of the myths in management is that higher employee pay results in higher employee performance. In about ninety percent of the cases, this is **not** true.

Wages and salaries have little to do with individual performance, once the pay is above the subsistence level. The primary reason for this is that pay received is not related directly to performance. About ninety percent of all employed people are paid according to time standards, not performance standards. Employees are paid by the hour, day, week, month, year, etc. rather than by what they do. It is implied that if an employee doesn't do enough satisfactory work, the employee is discharged; but the pay is not directly related to performance - especially in the minds of the workers.

About ten percent of the jobs in America are held by people

paid according to what they produce. Examples are sales people working on direct commission only and employees working on a one hundred percent piece rate plan. Here employees are paid directly according to what they produce. No performance - no pay!

The most highly motivated employees are those who are rewarded according to performance. One of the important rewards is money (pay).

As a new manager you can capitalize on this correlation by basing promotions and pay increases on **merit**.

How Do You Motivate?

New managers are interested in their employees' becoming highly motivated. Employees who are highly motivated are excited about their jobs, the objectives, the assignment, their responsibilities, the mission, etc.

People who are highly motivated tend to like what they're doing and have confidence they can do their jobs well. If employees are not highly motivated, the manager has a responsibility to stimulate them.

Since motivation comes from within a person, a manager cannot motivate someone else. What a manager does is inspire, stimulate, and enthuse employees to become more highly motivated.

The best technique to use to achieve this is to inspire someone positively about the importance of his or her job. Stress that the work is essential; emphasize the value of what each is doing and its importance to the department, the organization, and other employees; and generously recognize outstanding performance after the fact. Encourage outstanding performance to continue. Don't engage in negative stimuli such as coercion or threats of doom to get people motivated, even if it might work in the short run. Employees motivated by fear or from threats will leave an organization when they get a chance, and the effect on performance is short-lived at best. You are after permanent change and long-lasting results.

Motivation tends to be the highest when morale is high. Employees who have a good feeling about the importance of their work, their place in the organization, and their future normally will be highly motivated and satisfied.

The Rotten Apple Concept

Anyone who has ever seen a rotten apple in the middle of a barrel of good fresh apples knows that, in due time, the rotten apple will spoil the other apples unless removed.

The same holds true for employees who are dissatisfied, complain a lot, and are problem employees in general. If they are not removed, they will infect the employees around them.

Employees should not be dismissed to cover management's weaknesses. They should be dismissed only after their manager has tried sincerely every approach to correct, change, and improve their attitude and work performance. Some employees are in the wrong job and in the wrong company. Some employees bring outside problems to work, and these affect both performance and attitude. If problem employees do not respond after a reasonable period of time and effort, however, they should be dismissed.

You may have to don your gloves and become an "industrial surgeon" early in your management career, or you may never have to dismiss a problem employee. You cannot leave such an employee in the ranks without correcting the problem. To do so would be a disservice to the organization and to all of the productive employees.

The Danger of the Headless Chicken

Have you ever seen employees who run around and act like chickens with their heads cut off? They are the highly motivated employees who seem to have no direction, no visible goals, and yet are constantly in motion. A majority of these employees may be managers or staff personnel.

Somehow this type of employee is willing but not able. They may have ambition but no talent; they may have inspiration but no purpose. Some have ideas but no backing, or they have objectives but no plans. These employees are "dangerous" - much like a bull in a china shop.

Employees like the headless chicken type need direction, specifics, guidelines, and goals to become productive employees. Remember behavior of employees below you reflects on you as a manager.

Practice Personnel Preventive Maintenance

About ninety percent of all management problems involve people in some way. These may be employees, other managers, customers, suppliers, or others. Problems involving people are called general management problems.

A lot of time and effort is spent by managers on people problems. The practical approach is to try to prevent these problems before they occur. Anticipating many of these problems in advance requires a program of personnel preventive maintenance.

Companies budget millions of dollars annually for physical plant maintenance. Why not budget monies for personnel maintenance and avoid some of the human problems before they occur and cost even more? Such an expenditure should bring about a large return on investment.

A personnel preventive maintenance program requires management to organize a department or group for the sole purpose of continuously reviewing employee job needs, wants, and desires. Its objective would be to bring about complete job satisfaction among employees while insuring good employee performance, efficient operations, and increased loyalty to the company. It is a very good concept.

You as a manager can perform much the same function individually, in the absence of such an organized effort, by knowing your personnel and practicing effective leadership and communication techniques.

Above all, don't wait for a problem to develop; try to prevent it.

The Critical Factor in Personnel Selection

Every manager is involved in the personnel selection process. Even if your company has a personnel department to recruit, interview, process, test, and recommend personnel for employment, you as the manager should make the final decision regarding new employees.

Employees may be new to the organization, or they may be new to the department after transferring from within the company. In either case, there are always questions about new employees and their future job performance.

The process of selecting individuals for jobs in organizations is not scientific. You cannot guarantee successful work performance in advance of employment or promotion regardless of interviews, testing, references, etc. What you can do in the personnel selection process is weed out the applicants not highly qualified for a job. From the applicants left, the manager must make a judgment based on information available and a personal interview.

One point stands out. New managers should remember that the **best** indicator of future job performance is the record of performance in the past. This applies to everyone.

The difficulty is gathering accurate data about past performance. This is hard since information is not always readily available. Furthermore, a good record of past performance is still no **guarantee** of good future performance. But it is the best predictor available to the manager making the selection decision.

Keep the Objectives in Harmony

One of the important guiding concepts for new managers is the harmony of objectives concept. The idea is that a manager should so well know his or her individual employees that every day, as you work with these employees, you try to align their employee job needs, wants, and desires with the objectives of the organization.

The purpose of doing this is to create harmonious effort toward organizational objectives while satisfying individual employee's needs, wants, and desires on the job. Bringing this about on a daily basis requires much skill and insight on the part of the manager. The manager must know the values and aspirations of each employee and keep these in mind when delegating responsibility, controlling activity, and planning future work. Doing this successfully benefits the total organization.

The Overlooked Income

Most organizations proudly advertise their job openings and the accompanying wages or salaries. Advertising "fringe benefits" is not as common.

Fringe benefits go with the job and have now become approximately one third of the total wage bill. Most of the benefits provided an employee are paid for by the organization. Benefits may include health insurance, life insurance, workmen's compensation, some form of retirement or pension plan, social security, etc. Additionally, the organization may subsidize the food services provided to employees, may provide free parking, recreational facilities and equipment, reduced-cost vacation opportunities, pay part or all of the cost of advanced education, and many more things.

These benefits are expensive to provide; yet, most organizations do a poor job of selling these benefits to their employees as part of their income. The typical employee takes these things for granted and doesn't put into dollars and cents the value of receiving them. The company doesn't get any extra credit with employees for providing them with such benefits. This is why fringe benefits are often called the "overlooked" income.

You can sell these benefits to the employees and make them aware of the value they receive. Doing so becomes a real asset to the organization, and you will find the employees have a better attitude when they realize fully the changes in life style and standards of living these benefits make possible.

Put It in Writing

One of the true pearls of wisdom in management today says, "Put things of importance in writing."

In this world of legal relief for virtually everything it is essential to document in writing every event, reprimand, commendation, accident, etc. because organizations have many laws and legal regulations with which they must abide in the conduct of business. Nowhere is this more true than in the area of personnel - dealing with your employees.

As a manager, you will conduct performance appraisals, issue commendations and reprimands, counsel employees, hold departmental meetings, investigate problems and accusations, assign work, allocate any overtime necessary, receive instruction from your supervisors, and on and on. In all of these cases, you should record in writing the significant points that involve people, objectives, time standards, rule violations, and any other subject of importance.

It is essential to document in writing the performance records of your employees and their responses to your discussion of the evaluations. Whether the subject recorded reflects positively or negatively on an employee does not matter. Write it up and have the employee read the written statement and sign the document. The signature verifies that the report has been read and discussed and a copy given to the employee. File a copy and forward a copy to your supervisor, in addition to giving a copy to the employee.

Beyond the legal requirement to maintain documentation, it is simply good management practice to make written records of anything of importance that occurs in your domain.

Job Enrichment

Job enrichment is exactly what it implies. Managers have a chance, actually an opportunity, to enrich the jobs of employees if they are interested in increased employee job satisfaction. To enrich a job requires some creative thinking on the manager's part and from the employee as well.

Enriching a job does not mean changing performance expectations! It means changing the work environment, the flow of work, perhaps the job title, maybe introducing flex-hours, adding new and improved equipment, or a combination of things which will cause the employee to be more satisfied with his or her job. There is no formula to follow to bring about job enrichment. It is an individual effort to bring about better performance through more job satisfaction.

There is a strong tendency for employee performance to improve when job satisfaction is increased. Think about how you can enrich the jobs of your employees. Be empathetic as you plan methods of increasing employees' satisfaction through job enrichment.

The P and I Concept

The P and I Concept is the basis for the practice of participative management, which is the philosophy of management practiced in many American organizations today.

"P" stands for participation, and "I" stands for identification. The theory is that if you allow employees to participate in the actions or decisions affecting them, then they will identify with what takes place and be much more supportive of it and less resistant to it.

Possible additional benefits include increased organization loyalty, an improvement in employee self-esteem, more pride in work, a feeling of increased importance, and an overall improvement in morale. There is much merit to the P and I Concept, and many benefits can accrue to the manager who applies it properly. It can, however, backfire!

For example, if input from employees is requested on a proposal and the employees reject in advance what management wishes to do, management has created a major problem. To override employees' opinions will ruin the use of the P and I approach in the future. If management backs off on the proposed action because of employee rejection in advance, there is a question of who's running the organization!

Using the P and I approach carefully and properly can produce benefits. Perhaps the best way to increase employee participation and get positive results from P and I is through excellent one-on-one supervision. In this case, the manager - you

- gets the employee directly involved in changes, decisions, proposals, and suggestions; and in this way you can provide immediate positive praise and recognition for the employee's contribution.

The Job Dictates the Pay

In the vast majority of jobs in America (where people are employed by the hour, day, week, month, or year), the *job dictates the pay - not the person who holds the position.*

You will make a major management mistake if you allow employee pressure to influence the value of a job. Having a person perform a certain task every day or do a specific amount of work every day is worth just so much to the organization. It doesn't matter about the employee's sex, marital status, race, personal needs, problems, or ambitions. As long as the employee is doing the particular job, the pay is what the **job** is worth.

If the employee wishes to be paid more than he or she receives, then a promotion or transfer to a higher level **job** is necessary.

Pay rates need to be fair and equitable. Job evaluation is one approach to achieving this. Regardless of individual qualifications (experience and education), however, the job is worth only so much to the organization relative to the worth of other jobs being performed. That worth becomes the base pay.

Beyond this most organizations have merit increases, cost of living increases, and adjustments for seniority over and above base pay. A point of maximization is eventually reached in each job.

In managing, you must be sure that the employee fits both the work involved in the job and that the pay scale is appropriate. Don't waste your valuable time with an employee who expects the salary to be altered because of him or her. And remember an overqualified employee will most likely eventually become a troublesome employee.

The challenge is to match the right person to the right job.

About Planning and Control

Adopt Planning as a Way of Life

The basic process of management consists of planning, organizing, implementing, and controlling. It is a process because each function interrelates with the others; but planning is the first function of management and should precede the other three.

The activity of planning consists of looking ahead, generating ideas, establishing objectives, and working out all of the specifics before a plan of action is undertaken. The final plan should be in writing and it should state who does what, when, where, and how.

Sound planning before initiating action will not guarantee a problem-free course to reaching the objective. It is, however, an effort in advance to help you minimize problems and be prepared for those you can anticipate. Failure to plan carefully is the sign of poor management.

Rarely do managers overplan! On the contrary, most managers never come close to the point of diminishing returns for time spent in the planning stage. This would occur when the cost of planning exceeds the value of planning.

In general, you can say that the best planners tend to be the best decision makers, and the best decision makers tend to be the best managers.

The Number One Cause of Business Failure

Ineffective managerial planning is the number one cause of business failure and the number one reason why all organizational objectives are not achieved in the desired manner or in the desired time frame. Thousands of businesses fail each year. When you analyze why, the single most common and important reason is failure to plan adequately.

Planning is the key to sound decision making. Planning is the activity that looks into the future, anticipating problems, and formulating a course of action to reach your objectives efficiently and effectively with a minimum of problems.

Planning is one of the fundamental responsibilities of every manager. It is part of the job of being a manager. There is no way to avoid planning, whether you are good at it or not, if you are a manager.

Failure by management to look ahead, failure to prepare for problems, failure to control organized effort, etc. doom a project or an organization to ultimate disaster. Sound planning is the first step to achieving a successful end result.

Your charge as a new manager is to improve your planning skills immediately and constantly if you wish to succeed in management. You must make it so natural to analyze each step, project each alternative, evaluate each course of action to the fullest that you do these things without being consciously aware of it.

Strategy and the Planning Process

Sound planners follow a planning process before formulating a final plan of action. The planning process consists of subjects which must be considered and resolved before the final plan is implemented. The subjects to be considered are listed below, but it should be made clear that in practice some of these may not be of great value and others peculiar to the special situation may be added.

Planning is a nontheoretical, common-sense activity which everyone is involved in every day. Formal planning, however, should not be eliminated but emphasized as a necessary activity to bring about the best possible end results in the most efficient and effective way.

You should commit the following steps in the planning process to memory:

1. Generate ideas and review them.
2. Select the best idea and make it a working objective.
3. Research your objective.

4. Establish a time standard for achieving the objective.
5. Inventory resources (what you have on hand vs. what you need).
6. Review alternative ways of achieving the objective.
7. Determine a course of action.
8. Develop an organization structure for assignment of responsibilities.
9. Plan your program of coordination and control.
10. Consider the necessary organizational guidelines to direct and influence employee behavior.
11. Anticipate major problems in advance and prepare for them.
12. Blueprint your plan of action (put everything in writing).
13. Take action.
14. Follow up, review progress, and adjust plan as needed.

Once you have followed these steps and carefully considered what your objective is, then you have a written plan of action which is called a **strategy**. No subject is more current or of greater concern in today's organizations than "strategic management." It is simply carefully and thoroughly formulating your plan of action by following the planning process.

Generating Ideas and Objectives

Probably the most overlooked responsibility in management is that of generating ideas. Few organizations stress this as part of a manager's job. It is, however, and you as a new manager can get ahead by realizing it.

New ideas are the forerunners of new products, designs, work methods, advertising, product improvements, and hundreds of other things which make some organizations much more successful than others. A new idea can put additional revenue into the coffers or save money by cost-effectiveness. If the idea is yours, you have made your mark on top management.

Few people use more than five or ten percent of their creative ability. Yet, practically everything around us is wide open for improvement including the activities in any kind of organization.

The most successful organizations are filtering hundreds of ideas annually to bring about change and improvement. Some sponsor contests to encourage creative thinking. These organizations make changes by design - not by accident! Business firms like this encourage "fresh thinking," and they lead their industries.

You can find new ideas anywhere. There is no illegitimate source. You should use your creative ability to generate ideas yourself, learn to stimulate the creative talents of your employees, read trade journals, watch what competitors do, listen to customers, and keep up with technological advances. All are fertile sources for new ideas.

Once you have learned to generate and uncover ideas, you must differentiate between them until the best is selected. These best ideas in tangible form become the working objectives of the organization.

Set Time Standards at a Level of Excellence

One of the most important aspects of planning is to accompany objectives with a time standard. That is, the objective should be reached or achieved by when?

Many American managers are reluctant to have high expectations of employees. For this reason time standards are set too low - at a mediocre level rather than one of excellence.

Time is our most precious resource. It can be equated with money. Wasted time is a significant cost factor.

It becomes your job as a manager to put time in terms of dollars and to guard time as closely as if it were money.

Employees tend to do their best work when they know exactly what to do, why their work is important, and when it must be completed. Often, the last point is left out when delegating work. It is important to stress why the work must be completed by the deadline, too.

If you want employees to have high morale, stress the importance of their work and have them work against a time standard set at a level of excellence. When they achieve good results under these conditions, recognize them for outstanding work and continue the practice.

"Red Tape" Is a Sometimes Necessary Evil

"Red Tape" is a slang expression for organizational guidelines. An organizational guideline is defined as anything management introduces to influence the behavior of employees toward achieving objectives.

Organizational guidelines are introduced by managers as part of their planning responsibility. Examples of guidelines are rules, procedures, policies, systems, budgets, forecasts, and many more. Although each example can be defined differently, all guidelines qualify as something management introduces to channel employees' performance in a certain way.

It is costly to introduce red tape and costly to administer it. Most organizations are overloaded with red tape. Some of this may not be the fault of management, since the government may require a company to follow certain procedures and file forms, etc. But nearly every company has some red tape that is extraneous. How can you tell? Ask if the guideline consistently is followed, enforced, practiced, publicized, and reviewed. If any of these questions gets a "No" response, the red tape may be out of date.

As a general rule, the red tape in an organization should be kept to a minimum. Here are some suggestions to you for your implementation and use of red tape:

1.   Don't introduce any red tape unless it is considered absolutely necessary.
2.   If you introduce red tape, keep it simple.
3.   Put all red tape in writing and make sure all employees affected by it have a copy with a full explanation of the effect on them.
4.   Periodically audit red tape in your area of supervision and get rid of any that is no longer essential.

Use red tape when you need it. It saves you time as a manager by prescribing action or setting procedures for you to follow. You are relieved of having to evaluate each routine incident separately and know the limits you have in judging the situation. Be sure the guidelines are essential, and you are consistent in your use of them.

Be Aware of Both Risks and Uncertainties

The failure to anticipate major problems in advance is probably the number one planning weakness of most managers. When looking ahead and speculating about what might happen as you pursue objectives, you must be aware of **risks and uncertainties**.

An organizational **risk** is any event, occurence, or act that a manager ought to be able to anticipate and plan for. Doing this means that if the possible problem becomes a reality, you can offset or minimize the effect.

An **uncertainty** is any event, occurence, or act that a manager cannot anticipate nor plan for. If one of these occurs, the organization will either benefit by a windfall or be harmed (a disaster). But it does not relate directly to good or bad management.

Risks have to be calculated. That is, if a manager believes there is a reasonable probability an event will occur, such as a strike, managers should plan in depth and be prepared. If the probability is slight for such an event, the planning time invested in preparing for it is minimal or none.

Uncertainties are rare! Nearly everything that happens in the future which affects an organization's efforts to achieve an objective should have been uncovered, anticipated, and planned for. Failure to be ready for the obvious possibilities is inexcusable. An uncertainty encompasses such things as an earthquake in an area where no previous earthquakes have occurred or a terrorist bombing with no apparent reason and no prior activity to indicate such a thing might happen.

Often the single difference between the professional manager and the average (mediocre) one is the ability to anticipate and prepare for major problems in advance. Learn to examine every aspect and to acknowledge every possible problem. Then, master the habit of planning properly for each likely event.

Blueprint Your Plans of Action

Planning is the essential activity which helps minimize problems and reach objectives in an efficient and effective way. Sound planning, however, dictates that you put your final plans in writing.

Writing out exactly who is to do what, where, how, and at what time takes the guesswork out of the planning effort.

Much like an engineer who draws blueprints for a building project, a manager blueprints final plans. These plans can be copied, distributed to all parties involved, and discussed in depth before action begins. Having something in writing provides a road map for all to follow. This leads to coordinated effort; it minimizes wasted time; it gives direction to effort; it provides a standard for evaluating performance in progress; and it becomes an official document to alter in case plans are changed.

Remember, no plan is too small to put in writing.

Act and Evaluate

Planning precedes the action and action precedes evaluation.

Following a well-conceived plan should bring about more coordinated, efficient effort toward the achievement of objectives. This is the purpose of planning. Once the effort has taken place and the implementation of the plan is over, however, evaluation is the next step.

Only the best managers evaluate performance after the fact. The purpose of evaluation is to review all of the experience encountered in executing the plan. Note should be made of the strengths and weaknesses of the planned effort. You should learn from the experience so that an even better job can be done next time. This should take place even if the plan was implemented seemingly without a hitch.

Because of evaluation in depth after the completion of each

plan, time may be saved, new processes may be discovered, and bugs in new systems ironed out ahead of time, etc. in the next plan or the next phase of operations.

By being totally objective a manager can learn much from evaluating mistakes and successes. This should insure a more effective planning effort in the future.

Make Progress on Purpose

These are magic words for the successful organization!

Progress is made on purpose rather than by accident in the well-managed organization. If top management adopts this philosophy and it permeates the entire organization, all employees at all levels get the positive spirit for bringing about change.

Progress on purpose refers to attacking problems instead of retreating from them. It implies finding ways to improve rather than maintaining the status quo. It requires generating ideas and plans about the future rather than waiting for things to happen.

Great organizations have great management and leadership, and thus they have great employees. Great organizations always excel at doing something better than their competition. Part of the reason for this is the adoption of the philosophy that progress will be made on purpose. This requires full utilization of resources in the best possible way including brainpower and skillful planning on the part of management.

The Mysteries of Change

Nothing is more important to an organization than innovation or change. It makes the difference in competition for survival. But there are two facts about change that complicate its use for management.

Change in an organization refers to doing things differently from before. If change is to have a lasting effect, it will be authorized by top management and flow downward throughout the organization. Change is never lasting when introduced from below. Higher management must instigate it or approve it, and then introduce and endorse change for anything new and different to happen in the organization.

Bringing about change in the organization which improves work activity, the work environment, the morale of employees, or anything else is a responsibility of all managers. The problem is that employees generally resist change of any type.

A managerial decision designed to benefit employees will be subject to resistence just as much as if it benefitted customers, stockholders, and the general public at the expense of employees. Prepare the introduction of any change carefully to minimize this resistance. It is a true test of managerial effectiveness to institute change with a minimum of employee resistance.

Employees must be made aware of the value of the change. They must understand the importance of change and that it makes the organization grow and compete better.

You as a manager have the responsibility to prepare and educate your employees so well that they accept change and grow with the organization and with you.

Prioritize

Individual control of time is a necessity for managers who wish to be well-organized and get things done. One of the best ways to accomplish this is to set priorities before you act.

Determine which jobs and problems are really critical and concentrate your time and energy on them. By doing this, you can accomplish those tasks and resolve those issues which have the most significant "payoff."

Many activities in all organizations can be called "trivial." A manager should stay busy, but not busy handling trivia which would be quite easy for any manager to do. The difference is in end results. Trivia will not lead to obtaining the desired results for you or your organization. Avoid trivial activity at all costs. Use your talent, brain, and total energies when and where they count: where results can be measured and the objectives achieved.

Don't postpone acting on any important subject, no matter how distasteful the subject may be. Remember, be prompt to act and complete in accomplishing any undertaking. You can control your own management destiny by following this practice. Results are your goal since you will be judged on what you have accomplished. Stay tuned to the vital factors that lead to results and concentrate on them.

Control Programs

The main functions of managers are to plan, organize, implement, and control. Theoretically, if managers throughout the organization were perfect planners, organizers, and implementers, there would be no need to control. But when people are involved and there are risks and uncertainties about the future, there is a need to control activity.

How much control should management introduce in an effort to reach its objectives? Just enough and no more than necessary.

Control programs are expensive and tend to be negative because most control programs measure performance after the fact. If the control activity determines that a product being manufactured doesn't meet quality specifications, it is good to identify the problem, but the damage has been done. If at all possible control programs should be positive and preventive in nature rather than negative and corrective.

Control programs should never be introduced to cover up bad management or poor engineering.

Control programs are needed, but most organizations cannot afford nor justify excessive controls - "overkill." Control programs are part of red tape and should pay for themselves. That is, the value of the control program should exceed the cost of its implementation.

Traditional control programs have the same steps:
1. Set a standard.
2. Appraise performance against the standard.
3. Take corrective or remedial action when necessary.

In general, you can say that the primary purpose of all control programs is to measure performance against plans (standards) and keep all activity on track toward achieving the desired results.

About Organizing

What Is a Formal Organization?

A formal organization is where you work, the city, state, and Federal government, or perhaps a civic club to which you belong. Formal organizations have primary objectives, people in charge of other people, and a physical setting for a workplace.

The formal organization can be defined as a group of people who work together toward common objectives with clearly established lines of authority, responsibility, accountability, and communication.

Defects in the structure of the formal organization are the number one source of daily management problems. When work effort is disjointed, not very coordinated, and inefficient, then review the organization structure.

A breakdown in the proper order of things is no doubt the underlying cause of these problems. Work assignments, timing of effort, and synchronization of resources need to be reviewed to correct these problems and improve the organized effort.

Know Your Organization Structure

Most American organizations are structured as either *straight line* type or as *line and staff* type.

Most small organizations of fifty or fewer employees are structured as "straight line." This means that, except for a secretary or two, all employees are "line" employees - involved in those activities that have a direct bearing on the primary objectives of the organization. There are no staff personnel.

As the organization grows in size, a need develops for specialization in some areas for which the line managers lack training, knowledge, or time to perform. Thus, the need for staff specialists and the creation of a "line and staff" organization structure.

When you become a manager, learn your organization's structure. Determine which functions are line and staff and know who has authority and who doesn't.

The Difference Between Line and Staff Functions

New managers sometimes have difficulty distinguishing "line" from "staff" activities. The distinction is important because it affects the flow of authority, responsibility, accountability, and communication in the organization.

Line activities are those which are related **directly** to the attainment of the primary objectives of the organization. For example, in a business firm, sales, production, and finance are essential line functions. The business would not exist without these activities, and all relate directly to the profit and survival objectives. Employees in these departments are "line" employees.

Staff activities and staff positions are an outgrowth of needs of "line" managers. Whenever a line manager needs help because of a shortage of time, lack of specialized knowledge, absence of technical expertise, or desire for counseling or coordination assistance, staff positions are created under that line manager to fill the need. These staff positions will report only to the line manager which they serve. Pure "staff" personnel have no direct authority over line employees. They may act on behalf of a line manager, if instructed to do so, but they have no authority of their own. They contribute to the organizational objectives, but **indirectly**.

There are instances when "specialized staff" employees are given limited line authority. The conditions are usually a critical problem arising in their area of expertise, and they are given authority to act and correct the situation, in place of the appropriate line manager. Such examples as security personnel handling serious theft problems or quality control specialists working on a product defect come to mind. These cases are not too common, and the line authority given staff specialists is limited and only lasts until the crisis is over.

The factor to learn and remember is the limits of "staff" functions. Don't use "staff" employees improperly, and see that "staff" personnel do not usurp any line authority (maybe *yours*).

The Organization Chart

Not every formal organization has an organization chart. The chart is a picture of the formal organization and provides a new manager much information. If the chart is correctly drawn and current, it will show your position and the relationship of your job to every other job. Additionally, it shows your scope of authority and responsibility and your line of accountability to the position and person above you. The formal communication system follows the lines on the organization chart.

If names of people holding the various jobs are put on the chart, you have a way of identifying who does what in the organization. If positions are open, the chart will show this. You can also visualize your route of promotion on the chart.

All in all, an accurately drawn chart made available to all employees provides much information about the jobs, the interrelationships of people and work, the communication system, and who has authority and responsibility over what.

Information such as that provided by an accurate organization chart is invaluable to a new manager. Learn to understand the organization chart of your organization, and develop one for your area of responsibility. It will give recognition to your employees, providing them with a feeling of importance, and it will be useful in showing them how important they are to the organization as a whole.

The Informal Organization

We have defined the formal organization as a group of people who work together toward common objectives with clearly defined lines of authority, responsibility, accountability, and communication. Note that the first half of the definition refers to the grouping of people - employees - working together toward common goals. Among the formal group of employees in any kind of organization you will have what is called the "informal organization."

Identifying the informal organization is important to a new manager. Often the informal organization, led by informal leaders, is a persuasive factor in determining attitudes and morale of the employees. "Informal" simply means that the leaders and the employee associations do not appear on the formal organization chart and are not outwardly recognized by management. It is a major mistake, however, to overlook or underplay the power and influence of the informal organization.

Groups of employees who lunch together or socialize after work are examples of the informal organization. Each of these groups has its natural leader who consciously or not exerts much influence on the behavior and attitudes of other employees.

If these leaders are positive about the organization, the working conditions, the job benefits, etc., then much of this will rub off on the group members. The opposite holds true as well.

This is why a manager should quickly identify the natural leaders of the informal organization. After doing so, he or she should insure that these leaders are job satisfied, positive in attitude, and optimistic about the future. Done sincerely by the manager, this action can generate many fringe benefits to the organization and help minimize employee problems and conflicts in the future. It should not be overdone, however, and no new manager should allow these natural leaders to "blackmail" him or her into favoritism. Remember, the point is for you to use the informal group and its leader, not vice versa.

Two Tests of Managerial Authority

Authority - power - is a potent aspect of management. As soon as you assume your management position, you should activate your authority. This gives you power. But remember, your authority comes from the position you hold, not you personally. In a few cases, some managers, in time, try to acquire more authority than the position carries. Eventually higher management blows the whistle on them because they have overstepped their position. Other managers operate handicapped, without full power, because they never use all the authority inherent in their jobs.

In a normal managerial situation managers must be accepted by their employees, or they have no authority. Regardless of the authority of the position, if employees do not respond positively to direction by the manager, the manager has no authority. When an Army Captain says "Charge!" and the troops sit there, he has no authority! The same applies to the manager who gives his or her employees a directive and gets no action. Authority is theoretical in this case, not real. This is the first test.

The second test of real managerial authority is whether a manager is supported by his or her manager above. Regardless of the action taken by the lower manager, there needs to be backing from above to maintain real authority. Without this backing, the manager's authority is undermined and imaginary.

When you become a manager, learn to recognize the two tests of authority. Use the full authority that your position in management carries, but know the limits and stay within the boundaries.

Master the Art of Delegating

All managers assign work to employees. This is called delegating responsibility. Yet, assigning work in an effective way so that the results are satisfactory and timely is an art that many managers have not developed.

The technique of delegating responsibility effectively to one of your employees consists of three steps:

1. Tell the employee clearly **exactly** what he or she is to do. Repeat the instructions several times if necessary or write it out. Have the employee repeat his or her **understanding** of the instruction back to you for confirmation.
2. Tell the employee exactly **when** the work is to be completed.

3. Tell the employee **why** the work is important and **how** it relates to other work in the organization.

Employees do not get excited about unimportant work, nor do they work their hardest and best when there is no clear time to complete the work assignment.

Since all jobs and work are important and essential, stress the importance of each job and the necessity of doing work well and on time. The vast majority of employees will respond positively to this kind of direction if they know you are sincere.

Learn to Use Principles of Organization

Over the many years research has been conducted in the field of management, principles of organization have been developed to aid practicing managers. These principles are not rules or laws; rather, they are guidelines to help the manager with his or her organizational problems and questions.

Principles are designed to influence a manager's thinking not to dictate it. Principles of organization are useful and should be reviewed at the time of promotion when you review the organization structure. They are helpful when a company reorganizes or when a new project or new company starts. Knowing these principles can help a new manager develop expertise more quickly and gain confidence in his or her job performance with fewer years of experience.

All principles of organization have some validity, but here are eight which will be of real value to any practicing manager:

1. The Span of Control Principle
2. The Scalar Principle
3. The Unity of Command Principle
4. The Parity Principle
5. Management by Exception
6. Graicunas's Theorem
7. The Principle of Specialization
8. The Principle of Simplicity

When applied to your area of responsibility, these concepts

can make your job easier. Remember that flaws in the organization structure are your number one source of daily management problems. Learn to use these principles to your advantage in your daily practice of management.

The Span of Control Principle

Every new manager should recognize there is a **limit** to the number of employees you or any other manager can manage effectively. This is not a predetermined number. There is no magic number of employees to manage which minimizes conflict and problems. On the contrary, some individual managers may be able to supervise 25 employees effectively while others may have their hands full with three.

Factors which affect this span of control have been identified, though, and you must consider them as a manager:

1. The type of work being performed;
2. The type of workers performing the jobs;
3. The individual talent and skill of the manager, and
4. Physical factors such as noise, geographical distance, barriers, temperature, light, etc.

When a proven manager begins to have employee problems with turnover, overtime, low productivity, and complaints, it is a good idea to check the span of control of that manager. It may be that the limit of the number of employees the manager can supervise effectively has been exceeded.

As a new manager, be aware that there is a limit to how many employees any manager can supervise well. Know the factors that influence the limit for any individual, and learn to recognize the "people problems" that indicate you may be near or at your personal limit.

The Scalar Principle

This principle says that authority in the formal organization flows one link at a time from the top to the bottom. It is commonly called the Chain of Command Principle.

The value of this principle is to insure that higher managers go through the immediate lower manager to deal with employee problems under that manager. Also, it stresses that employees must go through their immediate supervisor before making contact with higher management.

Authority in the formal organization flows downward, and no employee below has any authority over employees above him or her.

One of the major sins in management is bypassing the formal positions of authority up and down the chain of command. If your superior allows your employees to by-pass you, both the manager and the employees have violated this principle.

Learn to go through the chain of command as a manager. Know your boss and the higher managers above your boss, but go through the proper channels and use the chain of command. Likewise, make sure your employees know you are open to their problems and suggestions and that they must go through you if they wish to deal with higher management.

The Unity of Command Principle

A somewhat old fashioned, but important, principle is **unity of command**. It says that no employee should report to more than one boss. In practice this principle is violated often; however, the question is, would the manager be more effective operating one on one rather than sharing employees with another manager?

From the employee's viewpoint, the question is, would he or she do a better job if only reporting to one manager with one set of requirements to satisfy? Too often in a situation of multiple accountability the employee is torn by conflict: Who's in charge of what? Who gets what time? Who do I go to for instruction?

If multiple managers have different sets of guidelines, expectations, demands, etc., the end result is waste because of poor productivity by a confused and often bewildered employee.

Unity of command resolves these problems. Overall there will be far fewer organizational problems if each employee reports to only one manager (boss).

If you are caught in one of the situations of multiple accountability, remember the employees' position. Take extra time to reassure the employees of whose expectations must be met on what part of their job. You must eliminate as much of the confusion and conflict as possible to keep productivity high and maximize efficiency.

The Parity Principle

Of all the organization principles perhaps the parity principle is violated more than any other. The parity principle states that authority and responsibility for results should be equal. That is, when a manager delegates responsibility to an employee, the manager should make sure that the employee has enough authority to get the job done.

As a manager you must be certain that when a task is delegated to you from above, you are given adequate authority to get the desired results. Having full responsibility and less than full authority to do a job guarantees frustration as well as probable failure.

Ask questions of higher management to determine the extent of the authority and responsibility delegated to you. And as a manager, when you delegate to your employees, provide the parity of responsibility and authority that will maximize results.

Management by Exception

When Moses led the people of Israel to the Promised Land, he had problems. Too much of his time was being spent dealing with every problem that developed. In talking with his father-in-law, Jethro, he learned the organization principle of management by exception. After he applied it and broke the group up into scores with leaders who handled the everyday problems, he was free to lead on and achieve the objective of the group.

Simply put, management by exception says that a higher level manager should not get involved directly with any of the problems or questions of a lower manager, unless the problem or question is so unique and so difficult that it is classified as an "exception." Then, timewise, it is justifiable to counsel with the lower manager and jointly arrive at a decision which the lower manager can implement. The decision then becomes the precedent for future problems of this type.

You should not confuse management by exception with being oblivious to what goes on in lower management ranks. It means that higher managers have their job to do and lower managers have theirs. Only when there is an "exceptional" problem, one without a precedent, can you justify taking a higher manager's time to resolve it.

Learn when to seek counsel from above and when to handle problems yourself. If there is no precedent for the situation, you had better consult your boss. If it is routine, keep the involvement to "for your information" only.

Too many **exceptions** may reflect badly on you as a manager and lead your boss to question your managerial ability and effectiveness.

Graicunas's Theorem

This principle gets its name from the management pioneer who developed it, V. A. Graicunas. It is also known as the *Principle of Increasing Organizational Relationships.*

The principle states that as you add people to an organization (or department), you do so arithmetically (1,2,3,4,5) but the organizational relationships that result increase geometrically (2,4,16,32,etc.).

The practical implication of this is that any organization adding a new activity, new product, new employee, or new department will find that the management problems associated with the addition increase at an enormous rate. You as a new manager will feel this effect by increasing something in your area of supervision by one - an employee, another machine, etc.

Growing may be the right thing for any organization. But managers must not overlook the point that growth in size and activity generates an extraordinary increase in management problems. These new problems must be anticipated in advance, and managers must plan and prepare for them.

Further, the value of any new activity, including your new

employee, must be far greater in value than the cost of the addition. Otherwise the action would be considered a bad management decision.

Remember this when you feel the need to recommend any type of increase in your area of managerial responsibility.

Principle of Specialization

The application of this principle in American industry is what made this nation great economically. The use of this principle is the backbone of mass production, low unit costs, and reasonable prices for manufactured goods.

The principle suggests that employees be trained and assigned to jobs where they can **specialize** and become masters of a particular work activity. By doing this a manager would have every job filled by highly trained people, and increased efficiency and productivity would result.

Intense specialization of work can make the difference in firms in highly competitive situations. But it can also result in employee problems.

Employees become bored and lose interest in their work, and the positive effects of specialization can be undermined. You must remember this if you manage workers who are specialized and keep them alert, involved, and interested in their jobs.

Principle of Simplicity

Despite the simplicity of it and the obviousness of it, this principle is one of the most important in organization. To a manager it means keep everything just as simple as possible. The value of simplicity cannot be overstressed.

For example, a manager should concentrate on the really important things when supervising people, not on trivia. Work processes should be streamlined around the essential activities. Red tape should be kept to a minimum. Employee talents should not be wasted. Control programs should be adequate but not excessive.

Unnecessary complexity in work activity is a waste of time,

effort, and money. It is your responsibility as a manager to pare activities continuously, and operate just as efficiently as possible.

Making Committees Productive and Exciting

The committee is a form of organization used by managers all over the world for many purposes. Committees can produce beneficial results, or committees can be a deterrent to progress and a waste of time. It all depends on the manager in charge.

Every new manager needs to understand how committees **should** function so that he or she can get positive and productive results if the opportunity arises to use or serve on a committee.

Needless to say, there are many kinds of committees. The most common are standing committees of an organization which tend to be permanent but have rotating membership. Other frequently used committees are called *ad hoc* and are created for a particular purpose and dissolved when the task is finished. The purposes of committees vary widely: safety, personnel practices, employee relations, finance, the office Christmas party, etc. Juries and boards of directors are examples of committees required by law.

Committees allow employees an opportunity to participate in decision making, and they spread the responsibility for action among the group. In addition, they pool the talents of many to provide ideas, research, and suggestions for the benefit of the organization. Sometimes a particularly vocal employee (who may be giving you trouble as a manager) can be turned into a positive influence by serving on a committee where he or she can have input and be taken seriously.

As a new manager you can use committees wisely by following these guidelines:

1. The members of a committee have to be highly qualified.
2. The committee needs to be properly "charged" by a manager who has respect and authority.

3. A highly qualified person should be elected or appointed "chair." This person must be a competent manager/leader who involves all committee members in the work and conducts the committee so that all members are positively motivated and recognized for their contributions.

4. When the work is completed, higher management should require a report and then act on it as well as show appreciation to all committee members for their efforts.

About Communicating

How To Be an Effective Communicator

Developing good communication skills requires practice. You are not interested in just passing along information, ideas, or facts to another person. You are interested in communicating **effectively**!

Effective communication means that the receiver (usually your employees) understands the message as you have intended; and the receiver responds, if necessary, as you desire.

Becoming an effective communicator suggests that you plan your communication and the techniques you will use before you act. Hasty communication is rarely effective. Professional managers also use empathy.

Empathy is putting yourself in the receiver's place. This is an important psychological technique which helps you better understand how to communicate effectively with another person or a group of employees.

Consider these suggestions for increasing your effectiveness as a communicator:

1. Know your subject thoroughly.
2. Plan your communication.
3. Empathize with the receiver before you act.
4. Develop a multifaceted communication approach.
5. Follow-up on your communication.
6. Learn from communication mistakes.

In addition, don't forget that communication is a two-way street. Listen to your employees, as well as your peers, bosses, and colleagues, give them your attention just as you expect them to do for you.

Barriers to Effective Communication

Problems in communication create more daily management problems than anything else. Part of the problem in communicating is that managers do not spot barriers to effective communication. Anticipating some of these barriers and trying to avoid them should allow a manager to be more effective as a communicator.

One barrier is the person who has a "closed mind." You've heard the expression, "Don't confuse me with the facts, my mind's already made up." Well, this is what many managers face in communicating. You must be creative in your approach with this type person, or you will never get your point or message through the barrier.

Semantics presents the second obstacle. Words have many different meanings, and you must be sure to use language, both written and verbal, that the other person will understand. It is best to simplify your message so that your intent will not be missed.

Third, some people jump to conclusions. These are the ones who have decided what you said before you finish expressing your idea or giving directions. Patience is the antidote for this barrier. Patience and repetition on your part will effectively overcome this problem.

Finally, you must have the attention of the person to whom you are communicating. Some employees are not alert or receptive to your verbal or written messages and appear lackadasical about their responsibilities. Often you have to require these people to repeat their understanding of the message back to you to be sure they get it straight. You nearly always have to follow-up on what you have said to them to make sure the correct response is made.

Any extra effort on your part in communicating costs time and money. But the cost of a mistake, an accident, a missed dealine, etc. is usually greater. As a new manager you can take no chances that what you are saying or writing to your employees is understood in the way you mean it to be one hundred percent of the time.

Use a variety of communication techniques. This will gain more attention from employees, and they will pay closer attention. Also, remember the cardinal communication principle: Your ability to communicate effectively varies directly with your knowledge of the subject. Specifically, know what you're talking about before you try to communicate.

Cross Communication

If you are manager "A" and have two employees, "B" and "C," do you allow them to communicate with each other about department problems? Do you allow them to communicate with other personnel in other departments on subjects of official business?

If you do, you are violating the chain of command principle of organization. "A" is the boss, is totally responsible, and will be judged on results. Why bypass "A"?

In daily practice in most modern organizations, "A" is bypassed regularly. The justification, **expediency**! Time is money and if a bypass results in faster action, why should you delay by going through "A"? The answer is you shouldn't; but two conditions have to be met to justify this cross communication.

First, the employee involved in cross communication must be doing something that is a legitimate part of his or her job. It is legitimate if "A" instructed the employee to do it; if it is part of the employee's job description; or if by traditional practice, this is what the employee is supposed to do.

Second, after condition one is satisfied, keep "A" posted. "A" or the boss of the cross-communicators must be informed about what's going on. It can be by memo, at staff meetings, by carbon copy, by telephone, stopping him or her in the hallway or parking lot, etc., but "A" must know what the employees are doing when they are involved in cross communication.

Never forget that as a manager, such as "A," you are totally responsible for everything from your position downward. You have to know what your employees are doing. Allow cross communication, but train your employees to keep you informed as a natural part of their communication process.

Make a Friend of the Grapevine

The informal communication system of the informal organization is called the "grapevine." Every organization of any size has a grapevine. Too many managers try to eliminate this informal communication system to no avail. Instead, managers should convert the grapevine into an asset.

To convert the grapevine, you use it. For example, tune into the grapevine. Listen to what's being communicated. Identify the "chief grape," that person who is always in the middle of the communication. This is an inexpensive way of evaluating morale, of finding out what's of real interest to the employees, and of keeping up with what's going on. The danger is that the grapevine has no conscience and communicates the untruths as readily as the truths.

Some managers have used the grapevine to distribute company information rather than calling meetings or sending out memos. The only problem with this is the risk that the information will be distorted as it is passed along.

The grapevine is fast, follows no formal lines of communication, and is available for all employees - management and nonmanagement alike - to use at no cost.

Accept the fact that the grapevine is here to stay, but learn to use it to your advantage as a manager when possible.

Downward and Upward Communication

Downward communication originates from higher levels of management and flows downward to lower levels. Downward communication can be an announcement to all employees over the public address system or the posting of important information on the bulletin board. Normally downward communication follows the chain of command (i. e., flows downward one level at a time without skipping any level) unless information is transmitted to all employees at one time. Downward communication tends to be faster than upward communication because of the status and authority associated with the sender. Downward communication is most effective when information is transmitted directly and personally to individuals, small groups and departments. It is least effective when the channel selected for transmission is indirect and impersonal. Examples of this are notices in the paycheck envelope, employee handbooks, and any form of "canned" communications directed to employees at lower levels.

Upward communication flows from lower levels of the organization to higher levels. Upward communication becomes effective if higher level managers encourage employees to communicate with them. Upward communication can be suggestions; ideas; responses to questions; reports on work completed, sales made and job problems encountered; and much more. Two major problems hinder the effectiveness of upward communication. One is the fear of employees that higher managers will not welcome their comments, suggestions or ideas, or that they will be misinterpreted in a negative sense. The second problem is that employees are not eager to communicate problems or bad news upward to higher managers.

Upward communication can be valuable to higher management in the following ways:

1. It can demonstrate the effectiveness of downward communication.
2. It can provide information on the progress and achievements of employees below.
3. It can transmit employee suggestions and ideas for improvement.
4. It can send signals to management above concerning employee morale and job satisfaction.